Facilitation at a Glance!

A Pocket
*Guide of Tools and Techniques for
Effective Meeting
Facilitation*

Written by
Ingrid Bens, M.Ed.
A joint publication of:

Facilitation at a Glance! is a condensed version of the popular manual entitled *Faciltiating with Ease!* which was written by **Ingrid Bens, M.Ed.** and published in 1997 by *Participative Dynamics.*

The *Association of Quality and Participation (AQP)* has joined forces with *Participative Dynamics* in the production of this pocket guide to provide continuing support for organizations' ongoing efforts to improve quality.

This pocket guide recognizes the growing importance of facilitation and aims to provide a comprehensive set of tools and techniques, in a simplified format, for anyone required to run meetings.

We hope you like our guide and will consider ordering one for everyone who attends meetings in your organization. Information about bulk orders is provided on pages 172 and 173.

Written by Ingrid Bens, M.Ed.
Edited by Michael Goldman, M.H.Sc.
Typesetting and Artwork by Mary House
Coordination by Geetha Balagopal, AQP

To **order** see pages 172 and 173, or call:

AQP Cincinnati, Ohio Phone: 800-733-3310	**Participative Dynamics** U.S.A – Sarasota, Florida 1-888-358-8848 or *Canada* – Toronto, Ont. 1-888-465-9494

Table of Contents

Introduction

*I*t's impossible to be part of an organization today and not attend meetings. Staff meetings, project meetings, task force meetings, coordinating meetings – the list is endless. The worst thing about many of these meetings is that they're poorly run and waste valuable time.

> *"Facilitation is fast becoming a core competency for anyone who's on a team, leading a task force, heading up a committee or managing a department."*

After twenty years of experience as a consultant, team leader and trainer, I'm totally convinced that its impossible to build teams, reach true consensus, or run effective meetings without highly devel-

oped facilitation skills. The good news is that these skills can be mastered by anyone!

This mini-book provides facilitation tools and techniques at a glance. It's a condensed version of the comprehensive manual on facilitation entitled *"Facilitating with Ease!"*

For information about ordering more *"Facilitation at a Glance"* books or for ordering *"Facilitating with Ease!"* see pages 172-173.

Ingrid Bens, M.Ed.,
Consultant and Trainer,
Participative Dynamics

Some Definitions

Facilitator:
One who contributes *structure* and *process* to interactions so groups are able to function effectively and make high-quality decisions. A helper and enabler whose goal is to support others as they achieve exceptional performance.

Content:
The topics or subjects under discussion at any meeting; also referred to as the task, the decisions made, or the issues explored.

Process:
The structure, framework, methods and tools used in interactions. Refers to the climate or spirit established, as well as the style of the facilitator.

Intervention:
An action or set of actions that aims to improve how a group functions.

Plenary:
A large group session held to share the ideas developed in separate subgroups.

Norms:
A set of rules created by group members with which they mutually agree to govern themselves.

Chapter 1
What Is Facilitation?

*F*acilitation is a way of providing leadership without taking the reins. A facilitator's job is to get others to assume responsibility and to take the lead.

What Does a Facilitator Do?

Facilitators make their contribution by

- helping the group define its overall goal, as well as its specific objectives
- helping members assess their needs and create plans to meet them
- providing processes that help members use their time efficiently to make high-quality decisions
- guiding group discussion to keep it on track
- making accurate notes that reflect the ideas of members
- helping the group understand its own processes in order to work more effectively
- making sure that assumptions are surfaced and tested
- supporting members in assessing their current skills, as well as building new skills
- using consensus to help a group make decisions that take all members' opinions into account
- supporting members in managing their own interpersonal dynamics

- providing feedback to the group members, so that they can assess their progress and make adjustments
- managing conflict using a collaborative approach
- helping the group communicate effectively
- helping the group access resources from inside and outside the group
- creating an environment where members enjoy a positive, growing experience while they work to attain group goals
- fostering leadership in others by sharing the responsibility for leading the group
- teaching and empowering others to facilitate

Differentiating Between Process and Content

The content of any meeting is what is being discussed: the task at hand, the subjects being dealt with, and the problems being solved. The content is expressed in the agenda and in the words that are spoken. Because it is the verbal portion of the meeting, the content is obvious and typically consumes the attention of the members.

Process deals with how things are being discussed: the methods, procedures, format and tools used. The process also includes the style of the interaction, the group dynamics and the climate that is established. Because the process is often silent, it is harder to pinpoint. It is largely unseen and often ignored in most meetings, as people are focused on the content.

Content	Process
What	**How**
The subjects for discussion	The methods & procedures
The task	How relations are maintained
The problems being solved	The tools being used
The decisions made	The rules or norms set
The agenda items	The group dynamics
The goals	The climate

Content vs. Process Leadership

A meeting leader offering an opinion with the intent of influencing the outcome of discussions is acting as the 'content leader.'

In contrast, a facilitator's job is to manage the process and leave content to the participants. When a meeting leader is neutral on the content and actively orchestrates the action, he or she is acting as the 'process leader' or facilitator.

Facilitation Behaviors & Tools

As a facilitator, you'll have an extensive set of behaviors and tools at your disposal. These fall into two categories: Core Practices and Process Tools.

The **Core Practices** define the manner, style and behaviors of the facilitator. Experienced facilitators:

- stay neutral
- listen actively
- ask questions
- paraphrase
- synthesize ideas
- use appropriate language
- manage digression
- offer clear summaries
- give and receive feedback

The effectiveness of any of these practices depends on how you handle yourself.

The **Process Tools**, which are structured activities that provide a clear sequence of steps, include the following:

- Visioning
- Brainstorming
- Nominal Group Technique
- Forcefield Analysis
- Gap Analysis
- Multi-Voting
- Priority Setting
- Root-Cause Analysis
- Decision Grids
- Systematic Problem Solving

Core Practices Overview

When facilitating you need to be constantly using the following core practices:

Stay neutral on content – Your job is to focus on the process role and avoid the temptation of offering opinions about the topic under discussion. You should use questions and suggestions to offer ideas that spring to mind, but never impose opinions on the group.

Listen actively – Look people in the eye, use attentive body language and paraphrase what they are saying. Aways make eye contact with people while they speak, when paraphrasing what they have just said and when summarizing their key ideas. Also use eye contact to let people know they can speak next and to prompt the quiet ones in the crowd to participate.

Paraphrase to clarify – This involves repeating what people say to make sure they know they are being heard, to let others hear their points a second time and to clarify key ideas. (e.g. "Are you saying ...? Am I understanding you to mean...?)

Ask questions – This is the most important tool you possess. Questions test assumptions, invite participation, gather information and probe for hidden points. Effective questioning allows you to delve past the symptoms to get at root causes.

Use the flip chart – This is another tool you should use constantly. It helps keep track of emerging ideas as well as final decisions. Notes should be brief and concise. They must reflect what the participants have said, not your interpretation of what they said.

Keep time – Appoint a timekeeper to call out time markers, or use a timer to help keep the group on track. Time guidelines need to be established for each item on an agenda. At first it may be distracting, but keeping track of time forces participants to stay focused.

Play Ping-Pong – Picture yourself standing at the flip chart with a Ping-Pong paddle in one hand. If someone asks a question or makes a comment, redirect it by sending it back to someone else to answer or build on. This is a great way to get participants to interact with one another. (e.g. "Sally, how would you answer the question Bill has just posed to me?")

Test Assumptions – You need to bring the assumptions people are operating under out into the

open and clarify them so that they are clearly understood by everyone. These assumptions may even need
to be challenged before a group can explore new
ground. (e.g. "John, on what basis are you making the
comment that Bob's idea is too narrow in focus'?")

Synthesize – Don't just record individual ideas of
participants. Instead, get people to comment and build
on each other's thoughts to ensure that the ideas
recorded on the flip chart represent collective thinking.
This builds consensus and commitment. (e.g. "Alice,
what would you add to Jeff's comments?")

Hold up a mirror – Periodically tell the group how
they look to you so that they can interpret their actions
and make corrections. (e.g. "Two people have not said
anything for ten minutes and three other people are
reading memos. What's this telling us we need to do?")

Summarize periodically – A great facilitator listens
attentively to everything that is said, and then offers concise and timely summaries. Summarize when you want
to revive a discussion that has ground to a halt or to
end a discussion when things seem to be wrapping up.

Label sidetracks – It's your responsibility to let the
group members know when they're off-track. They can
then decide to pursue the sidetrack, or stop their current discussion and get back to the agenda. (e.g. "We are
now discussing something that isn't on our agenda. What
does the group want to do?")

Park it – At every meeting, tape a flip-chart sheet to
a wall to record all sidetrack items. Later, these items

can be reviewed for inclusion in a future agenda. 'Parking lot' sheets let you capture ideas that may be important later, while staying on track.

Use the spell-check button – Most people are nervous enough about writing on flip charts without having to worry that they're spelling every word right. You will relax everyone by drawing a spell-check button at the top right corner of every flip sheet. Tell participants they "can spell creatively, since pressing the spell-check button automatically eliminates all errors."

Focus on Questioning

Effective questioning is the key facilitative technique. As a facilitator, you can never ask too many questions.

IF YOU WANT TO ...	THEN...
Stimulate everyone's thinking	Direct question to the group
Allow people to respond voluntarily or avoid putting an individual on the spot	Ask a question such as "What experiences have any of you had with this problem?"
Stimulate one person to think and respond	Direct the question to that individual. "How should we handle this Bill?"
Tap the known resources of an "expert" in the group	Direct the question to that person "Mary, you have a lot of experience...What would you do?"

Effective questioning means:
   Asking the right questions at the right time
Select the right type of question and phrase it so that it solicits the best possible response. Then, direct it to the right person.

Sample Probing Questions

The following sample questions are designed to delve more deeply into a problem situation.

- How would you describe the current situation in this department?
- How would your most important customer describe it?
- How would a senior manager describe it?
- How long has this situation been going on?
- How do you feel about the situation?
- Why hasn't the problem been solved?
- Who wants change to take place? Who does not?
- Who contributes to the problem?
- How do you contribute to the problem?
- If the problem were totally resolved, what would the situation look like?

On a scale of 1 to 5, how serious would you say this problem is?

1	2	3	4	5
not serious at all		somewhat serious		very serious

- What are the most significant barriers to solving this problem?

- What are the parameters of this initiative? (time, money, materials)
- Are any solutions going to be taboo or unacceptable?
- How would you rate the overall level of commitment to making changes that have been agreed to?

1	2	3	4	5
Low		Medium		High

Questioning: Do's and Don'ts

DO ...	DON'T...
Ask clear, concise questions covering a single issue	Ask rambling, ambiguous questions that cover multiple issues
Ask challenging questions that will stimulate thought	Ask questions that don't provide an opportunity for thought
Ask reasonable questions based on what people know	Ask questions that most people can't answer
Ask honest and relevant questions	Ask "trick" questions designed to fool them

The Language of Facilitation

A particular style of language has evolved as a part of facilitation. These techniques are especially important when it comes to commenting on people's behavior without sounding critical or judgmental. The main language techniques are as follows:

- paraphrasing
- reporting behavior
- describing feelings
- perception checking

Paraphrasing involves describing, in your own words, what another person's remarks convey.

> *"If I understand you correctly, you are saying..."*
> *"Is this an accurate understanding of your point...?"*
> *"What you are saying is..."*

You should be paraphrasing continuously, especially if the discussion starts to spin in circles or if people are getting heated. This repetition assures participants that their ideas are being heard. New facilitators often make the mistake of not paraphrasing enough.

Reporting behavior consists of stating the specific, observable actions of others without making accusations or generalizations about them as people or attributing motives to them.

> *"This is the third time you have rolled your eyes while I was presenting my ideas."*
> *"Two of you are reading and the others have grown very quiet."*

By describing specific behaviors you give participants information about how their actions are being perceived. Feeding this information back to participants in a non-threatening manner opens the door for individuals to suggest actions to improve the existing situation.

Descriptions of feelings consists of specifying or identifying feelings by naming the feeling, using a metaphor, figure of speech, or action urge.

> *"I feel exhausted." (naming)*
> *"I feel like a kid on vacation." (metaphor)*
> *"I feel like a fly on the wall." (figure of speech)*
> *"I feel like jumping for joy!" (action urge)*

As a facilitator, you need to be in touch with how you're feeling and not be afraid to share those feelings with the group. It is very helpful to be honest with a group by telling them "I feel exhausted right now," or "I feel frustrated." This lets other people know that it's okay for them to express feelings.

Perception checking is describing what you perceive to be another person's inner state in order to check if you understand what they are feeling.

> *"You appear upset by the last comment that was made. Are you?"*
> *"You seem impatient. Are you anxious to move on to the next topic?"*

Perception checking is a very important tool. It lets you take the pulse of participants who may be experiencing emotions that get in the way of their participation.

How Neutral Do Facilitators Really Need To Be?

One of the toughest challenges as a facilitator is staying neutral.

While your objective is to focus on process and stay out of content, there are three techniques that you can use to give direction without compromising your neutral role.

1st Strategy – Ask Questions

If you have a good idea that might help the group, don't withhold it. Instead, offer the idea as a question. For example, you can ask "What are the benefits of renting new computers as an interim strategy?" The group can then consider this option and accept or reject it. Your neutrality is maintained because you're not actually telling the group what to do. They still have the final say.

2nd Strategy – Offer Suggestions

Sometimes you'll have a good idea that the group has not considered, yet even when you pose it as a question it fails to make an impression. At this point, it's appropriate to ask the group to consider a suggestion from you. You might say: "What about exploring the potential of renting computers for the next six months, until your new budget is approved?" Although this might sound as if you've strayed into content, it's still facilitative as long as it sounds and feels like an offer, not an order. As long as the members retain the power to decide the issue, all you've done is help provide a new idea for their consideration.

3rd Strategy – Take off the Facilitator's Hat

If the group is about to make a serious mistake, and all of the questioning and suggesting in the world hasn't worked to dissuade them, you may need to step out of your neutral role and tell the group what to do. In cases like these, it's important to first signal that you're stepping out of the facilitator role and clearly state that you are now offering advice. You might say: "I need to step out of the role of facilitator for a minute and point out that renting computers is three times more cost effective than buying and doesn't stick you with outmoded hardware." This role shift is legitimate only if you truly believe that the group is in grave danger of making a major mistake and you absolutely have to help them. Be careful though: leaping in and out of the facilitator's role too often causes confusion and distrust. Taking off the hat should be done very selectively and cautiously.

Best and Worst Facilitator Practices

Some of the best things that a facilitator can do:
→ carefully assess the needs of the members
→ probe sensitively into people's feelings
→ create an open and trusting atmosphere
→ help people understand why they are there
→ view yourself as servant of the group's needs
→ make members the centre of attention
→ speak in simple and direct language
→ work hard to stay neutral
→ display energy and appropriate levels of assertiveness
→ champion ideas not personally favored
→ treat all participants as equals

→ stay flexible and ready to change direction if necessary
→ make notes that reflect what participants mean
→ listen intently to understand totally what is being said
→ periodically summarize a complex array of ideas so that they form a coherent summary
→ know how to use a wide range of discussion tools
→ make sure every session ends with clear steps for the next meeting
→ ensure that participants feel ownership for what has been achieved
→ end on a positive and optimistic note

Some of the worst things a facilitator can do:
→ remain oblivious to what the group thinks or needs
→ never check group concerns
→ not listen carefully to what is being said
→ lose track of key ideas
→ take poor-flip chart notes or change the meaning of what is said
→ try to be the centre of attention
→ get defensive
→ get into personality battles
→ put down people
→ unassertively manage conflict
→ let a few people or the leader dominate
→ never check how the meeting is going
→ be overly passive on process
→ push ahead on an irrelevant agenda

- → have no alternative approaches
- → let discussions get badly sidetracked
- → let discussions ramble without proper closure
- → not knowing when to stop
- → be insensitive to cultural diversity issues
- → use inappropriate humor

Facilitator Behaviors and Strategies

Regardless of whether you're a facilitator from inside the group or out, the team's leader or a member, the following are parameters for facilitator behaviors.

Be Informed – Successful facilitators always gather extensive data about their prospective participants in order to fully understand both their business and their needs. They survey and interview participants, read background reports and use prepared questions to build a complete picture of the group's situation.

Be Optimistic – Facilitators do not allow disinterest, antagonism, shyness, cynicism or other negative reactions to throw them off. They try, instead, to focus on what can be achieved and to draw the best from each participant.

Be Consensual – Facilitation is fundamentally a consensus process. Facilitators always strive to create outcomes that reflect the ideas of all participants equally.

Be Flexible – Successful facilitators always have a process plan for all meetings, yet at the same time must be ready to toss it aside and change direction if that's what is needed. Really great facilitators bring alternative strategies and possess a good command of process tools.

Be Understanding – There are great pressures on employees in today's workplace. Facilitators need to understand this and recognize that antagonistic or cynical behaviors are a result of high stress levels.

Be Alert – All great facilitators are expert people watchers. They pay careful attention to group dynamics and notice what's going on at all times. All process leaders need to train themselves to be watchful of how people interact and how well they are achieving the task.

Be Firm – Good facilitation is not a passive activity. It often takes a substantial level of assertiveness to keep people and activities on track. Facilitators should be ready to step in and direct the process if the situation calls for it.

Be Unobtrusive – The facilitator should do as little talking as possible. The participants should be doing all of the talking. The facilitator says only enough to give instructions, stop arguments, keep things on track and sum up. Trying to be the centre of attention or make yourself look important is a misuse of your position.

Special Note:

Facilitating should be an egoless activity. The purpose is to make the group succeed, not to make you look really important and clever. An effective facilitator will leave a group convinced that "We did it ourselves!"

Practice Feedback Sheets

An excellent way of getting better at facilitating is to ask a colleague to observe you in action and then give you feedback. On the next page is an observation sheet for feedback purposes. It focuses on core facilitation practices that are essential process requirements for any meeting. In using this sheet, the following feedback process can be helpful:

1. First have the facilitator talk about how he or she felt he or she did. Ask, "What did you think were your strengths? Weaknesses? What do you think could be improved?"

2. Next, have the observer offer specific descriptions of all the things he or she noted that you did effectively.

3. Finally, have the observer provide concrete suggestions for improvements that he or she believe would enhance your facilitation effectiveness.

Facilitation Core Practices Observation Sheet

✎ **Facilitator:** | **Observer:**

Behaviors that Help
- __ listens actively
- __ maintains eye contact
- __ helps identify needs
- __ gets buy-in
- __ surfaces concerns
- __ defines problems
- __ involves everyone in the discussion
- __ uses good body language & intonation
- __ paraphrases continuously
- __ provides feedback
- __ accepts and uses feedback
- __ checks time and pace
- __ provides useful feedback
- __ monitors and adjusts the process
- __ asks relevant, probing questions
- __ keeps an open attitude
- __ stays neutral
- __ offers suggestions
- __ is optimistic and positive
- __ manages conflict well
- __ takes a problem-solving approach
- __ stays focused on process
- __ Ping-Pongs ideas around
- __ makes accurate notes that reflect the discussion
- __ looks calm and pleasant
- __ is flexible about changing the approach used
- __ skillfully summarizes what is said
- __ knows when to stop

Behaviors that Hinder
- __ oblivious to group needs
- __ no follow-up on concerns
- __ poor listening
- __ strays into content
- __ loses track of key ideas
- __ makes poor notes
- __ ignores conflicts
- __ provides no alternatives for structuring the discussion
- __ gets defensive
- __ puts down people
- __ no paraphrasing
- __ lets a few people dominate
- __ never asks "How are we doing?"
- __ tries to be centre of attention
- __ lets the group get sidetracked
- __ projects a poor image
- __ uses negative or sarcastic tone
- __ talks too much
- __ doesn't know when to stop

Chapter 2
Facilitation Stages

*O*ne of the biggest mistakes you can make as a facilitator is to show up at a meeting without having assessed the situation or prepared design notes for the session. Before you facilitate any meeting you should be aware of the specific stages involved to ensure proper planning and implementation.

While the following steps are most often followed by an external facilitator, these steps can also be used if you're an internal person who is asked to plan and run a complex meeting or workshop. Note that steps 4, 5 and 6 are useful in facilitating any small group discussion.

Stages in Conducting a Facilitation	
1. Assessment and Design	
2. Feedback and Refinement	
3. Final Preparation	
4. Starting a Facilitation	Applicable
5. During a Facilitation	steps for any
6. Ending a Facilitation	meeting
7. Following up on a Facilitation	

1. Assessment and Design

The first step in ensuring success in any facilitation is to make sure the meeting design is based on detailed information about the group.

The best way to start is by interviewing the person who asked you to conduct the meeting. It's important to also gather information from at least a few other members. Always check your assumptions, and theirs, by gathering data from a cross section of members. There is nothing worse than basing the design of a meeting on what the leader has told you, only to find that no one else in the group agrees with that assessment.

You can use one or more of the following techniques:

- one-on-one interviews
- group interviews
- surveys
- observations

Samples and details of each technique are included in ChapteR 3, starting on pg. 33.

Any time you gather data about a group, a summary of that information must always be fed back to the group. This can be done by providing the members with a written summary of the assessment notes or by writing key points on a flip chart and reviewing them briefly at the start of the session.

If possible, share this feedback before the meeting agenda is presented. If you've done a good job, the design of the meeting should sound like it flows directly from the information gathered.

Once all the data is in and you feel confident that you understand the group and their needs, you can create a preliminary design. This includes identifying the objectives of the session and writing an agenda with detailed process notes. Refer to pg. 111 for information about developing process notes.

2. Feedback and Refinement

Once you've created a detailed agenda for the session, it's wise to share that design with group members and get their input and approval.

If your design is intended for a large group, or a complex event, this feedback activity will need to be more formal. It's common to meet with a workshop team of two or three group members so that they can hear the feedback from the data gathering and review the proposed design being presented. If the design is for a smaller, less complex meeting it's fine to discuss your agenda ideas with the leader and/or representative member.

There are many situations in which the group's members may not like what you've designed. There's often a gap between what a group wants and what the facilitator thinks it needs.

If a disagreement about the design arises, you need to ensure that all viewpoints are heard and that optional designs are considered. If the group has valid reasons for not wanting to do an exercise (i.e. the content is too sensitive to discuss, the objectives have changed, etc.), respect that concern.

On the other hand, you should stand firm and assertively promote your design, especially if meeting members are new or reluctant to use participatory techniques or have a history of dysfunction. Listen to their objections, then help them understand your recommendations. What they want is not always what they need.

Once agreement on a final workshop design has been reached, you can write a brief summary of both the feedback and final version of the design and send it to the group's representatives. This written memo will help reduce the potential for misunderstanding.

3. Final Preparation

Professional facilitators spend as much time preparing for a facilitation session as they do leading the actual event. The industry standard for session leaders is one day of preparation for each day of facilitation. Some complex sessions even have a ratio of two days of preparation for each day of facilitation.

Here are common time allocations for facilitation assignments:

Workshop Length	Interview Time	Design Time	Total Time
I day workshop (18 people)	1/2 day	1/2 day ➡	2 days
2 day workshop (18 people)	I day	I day ➡	4 days
2 day retreat (60 people)	I day	3 days ➡	6 days

What you, the facilitator, should do as part of the final preparation:

- finalize the design and put it in writing for the client
- clarify the roles and responsibilities of all parties
- check the suitability of the meeting location
- help the group leader prepare a letter detailing meeting logistics and the final agenda
- identify all materials and supplies required
- design and write all workshop materials and handouts
- complete all overheads and required flip charts

The members of the group are typically responsible for sending letters to other members, arranging and paying for all logistics such as meals and accommodations, ensuring that a suitable meeting room is available, arranging and paying for printing, making sure members attend, keeping clear minutes of the proceedings, transcribing all flip-chart notes, monitoring to ensure follow-through on all action plans and evaluating the results.

4. Starting a Facilitation

As the facilitator, you should always be the first person to arrive for any meeting. This ensures that there is time to make last-minute seating changes in the meeting room, post the agenda and survey data, test the equipment and so on.

Room setup is critical for sessions. A large room with modular furniture works best for both large group and subgroup settings. Huge boardroom tables, on the other hand, are detrimental to creating an atmosphere conducive to dialogue. A long table also tends to reinforce hierarchical patterns and discourage eye contact between members.

When facilitating large groups it is best that you seat the attendees at round tables spaced evenly around the room. Small table groups consisting of between five to eight persons are ideal.

Make sure there is ample wall space for posting the flip-chart sheets that will be generated throughout the day. Lots of easels are usually needed; order one for each subgroup and two for the front of the room.

Chatting informally with members as they arrive not only helps break the ice, it gives people an opportunity to get to know you.

You'll develop your own personal approach for beginning a session over time; however, this one will help you get started:

__ introduce yourself and give a brief personal background
__ clarify the role you will play as the facilitator
__ clarify the roles to be played by any other members
__ go around the room and have members introduce themselves by name and perhaps position, especially if there are people present who don't know each other

- __ conduct a warm-up activity to relax the group; make sure this fits with the time available and activity focus
- __ review any data collected from members; have key points written on flip chart paper or on overheads; answer questions
- __ clarify the goal and the specific objectives for the session
- __ review the agenda and invite comments; make any changes
- __ specify time frames; appoint a timekeeper; make sure there is true acceptance of the agenda
- __ take care of all housekeeping items
- __ get the group to set norms for the session by asking "What rules should we abide by during this meeting?"
- __ post these norms on a wall within clear view
- __ set up a parking sheet to keep track of digressions for later review
- __ proceed to the first item on the agenda; make sure everyone is clear about what's about to be discussed
- __ explain the process, or how you will be handling this agenda item
- __ be sure that the time frame for the first item is set; have a timekeeper and a minute taker
- __ begin the discussion

5. During a Facilitation

Your key contribution during any meeting is to provide the structure and process focus that will keep the discussion moving efficiently and effectively.

You'll need to the following:

✎ __ ensure that all members participate
__ manage conflicts
__ keep the group on topic
__ 'park' off-topic items
__ help members adhere to their ground rules
__ make interventions if there are problems
__ maintain high energy level
__ set a positive tone
__ keep track of the discussion by making concise notes
__ get on with the discussion

As a meeting proceeds, periodically employ the following process checks:

Check the pace — Ask members how the pace feels to them:

"Is this session dragging or are you feeling rushed?
What can we do to improve the pace?"

Respond to their assessments by implementing needed adjustments.

Check the process — Periodically ask members if the approach being taken is working

"We said we would work this issue through as a

*large group, rather than as a subgroup. Is this
approach working or should we try something else?"*

Adjust the process throughout the session to ensure
that things keep working.

Take the pulse of members — Continuously read
faces and body language to determine how people are
feeling. Don't hesitate to ask

*"How are members feeling? Do we need a stretch?
Is anyone feeling like they have dropped out? How can
we get our energy levels up again?"*

'Reading' people lets you know when to stop for a
break or bring lost members back into the fold.

Summarize — When there are lots of ideas floating, summarize what's being said. Stop and review:

"Let's see what we've got so far."

If the discussion seems to be winding up:

*"Let me read what we've said to see if we've
reached a conclusion."*

Summarizing helps people who might have lost track
of the conversation get back in. It can revive a group in
a slump or help move the group toward closure.

6. Ending a Facilitation

One of the most common problems in any meeting is
lack of closure. Lots of things get discussed, but there's
no clear path forward. One of your key contributions is
to ensure that decisions are arrived at and detailed
action steps are in place before the group adjourns.

Here are some ways you can help a group bring effective closure to a meeting:

✎ __ make clear statements about what has been decided and write these decisions on a flip chart

__ ensure that they have created detailed action plans with names, accountabilities and dates beside each step

__ round up items not discussed at the meeting, including those on the 'parking lot' list, prioritize them, and create plans to deal with them in future

__ create an agenda for the next meeting

__ decide on a means for follow-up, either written reports or a group session

__ help members decide who will take all the flip-chart sheets for transcribing

__ conduct a written evaluation of the session

__ solicit personal feedback from participants

__ allow members to express how they felt about the session

__ clarify your role in the follow-up process

Once the session is over, thank the participants for having you facilitate and help clean up.

7. *Following up on a Facilitation*

No matter how formal or informal the facilitation process has been, a follow-up with the group is always a good idea. If the facilitation consisted of a brief meeting, you might simply call the group leader to determine the extent to which the session helped the group become more effective.

If the session was a major decision-making workshop or retreat, encourage the group leader to send out a written follow-up questionnaire to the members.

Unless it was formally agreed that you would conduct the follow-up activity, you can leave any post-session reports to the group's members. This ensures that they, not you, assume accountability for the implementation of the ideas emerging from the session. Your role may be to merely remind the group about the need for a follow-up and to provide them with a format for reporting results later.

In some cases you may negotiate with the group to facilitate a follow-up meeting at which the progress is discussed and evaluated.

Chapter 3
Knowing Your Participants

Getting to know the people you'll be working with is an essential first step in designing effective meetings. Before you facilitate you need to know if they are the following:

  __ total strangers who have never met before and won't be together again after this single special-purpose meeting

  __ total strangers or people who have only a passing acquaintance with each other, but who will be working together again after this meeting

  __ a group of people who know each other, have interacted for some time and get along well

  __ a group in turmoil who meet periodically and either spin their wheels in frustration or get embroiled in conflicts that are rarely resolved

  __ a high-performance team with a solid track record of achievements, made up of members with highly developed people skills who are good at managing group dynamics

Conducting an Assessment

Never take a group or situation for granted. It's up to you to carefully read a group and design a process that matches their circumstances.

To get the information you need, try one of these approaches:

- **One-on-one interviews** allow you to question people about the state of the team and member interactions. This is the best way to get people to open up and be candid when there are sensitive issues in the group.

- **Group interviews or focus groups** are a good strategy when the subject isn't overly sensitive and/or there are too many people to interview singly. Group interviews let you observe the group's interpersonal dynamics before the actual facilitation session.

- **Surveys** let you gather anonymous information from all members. They enable you to compile answers to the same questions from each member. They also generate quantifiable data.

- **Observing the group in action** helps you understand the interpersonal dynamics. This involves sitting on the sidelines during meetings in order to get a sense of who plays which roles and how people relate to each other. It is very useful if the team is in conflict.

Assessment Questions

When meeting a new group, you will need to ask certain questions to determine the state of the group.

- What's the history of the group?
- How familiar are members with each other?

- Are there clear goals?
- Are there team norms or rules?
- Does everyone participate or do a few dominate?
- To what extent are members honest and open?
- Do members listen to and support each other's ideas?
- How does the group handle any conflicts?
- How are important decisions made?
- Do people leave meetings feeling like something has been achieved?
- How would you describe the group atmosphere?
- Are meetings thoroughly planned and structured or are they basically freewheeling?
- Does the group ever stop to evaluate how it's doing and make corrections?
- What's the best thing about the group? What's the worst?
- How do people feel about being on this team?
- Describe a recent incident that illustrates how members typically interact.
- Are there any reasons why members might not be open and say what they really think?
- Why do you need (external) facilitation support? Is there any opposition to this?
- What is the worst thing that could happen at this meeting? What could be done to ensure that this doesn't happen?

These questions are presented in survey form on the next page.

Group Assessment Survey

1. How familiar are members of this group with each other?

1	2	3	4
Passing acquaintances	We work together	We're a team	We are a high-performance team

2. Are there clear goals for the group?

1	2	3	4
We have no stated goals	Not sure about the goals	Fairly sure about the goals	Clear goals we set ourselves and monitor

3. Does the group have a clear set of rules to manage interactions?

1	2	3
No rules exist	There are norms but they aren't used effectively	We have and use rules that we created

4. Describe the typical participation pattern?

1	2	3
A few people dominate consistently	Participation varies from topic to topic	Everyone plays an equal role

5. How much honesty and openness is there in this group?

1	2	3	4
People hide what they really think	We are somewhat open	We are quite open	We are totally open and honest

6. How good are members at listening, supporting and encouraging each other?

1	2	3	4
We don't do this at all	We try but don't always succeed	We are fairly skilled at this	We are consistently excellant

7. How do members typically handle differences of opinion?

1	2	3
No rules exist	There are norms but they aren't used effectively	We have and use rules that we created

8. How are important decisions usually made?

1	2	3	4
One person decides	Vote	Seek compromise	Work together to reach consensus

9. Does the group usually end its meetings with a sense of achievement and clear action plans?

1	2	3	4	5
Never	Rarely	Sometimes	Usually	Always

10. How would you describe the atmosphere between members?

1	2	3	4
Hostile and tense		Satisfactory and harmonious	Totally relaxed

11. How would you describe the group's meetings?

1	2	3	4
Unstructured, a waste of time		So-so	Well planned and productive

12. Does the group ever stop and evaluate how it's doing, and then take action to improve?

1	2	3	4
Never	Rarely	Sporadically	Consistently

Chapter 4
Creating Participation

*I*magine yourself at the start of a day-long session with a group of people you barely know and nothing is working. No one is answering questions. Some people look bored. Others seem openly uncomfortable. Everyone looks nervously at the leader whenever you ask a serious question. You start to wonder how you're going to get through the rest of the session!

Your first step in getting people to participate actively is to understand why they're exhibiting non-participatory behavior.

Consider these main barriers to participation:

- ___ members may be confused about the topic being discussed
- ___ there may be a lack of commitment to the topic under discussion
- ___ they may feel unsure about the quality of their personal contribution
- ___ they may be insecure about speaking in front of others
- ___ they might be afraid of the reaction of their peers
- ___ talkative members may 'shut down' quieter people

- some people may be reluctant to speak up in front of those they consider to be their 'superiors'
- there may be a low level of trust and openness in the group
- some traumatic event may have occurred recently that has left some members feeling withdrawn
- the organization may have a history of not listening to or supporting employee suggestions

When planning any session, it's important to assess how participative the members are likely to be. You can do this before the workshop begins by finding out the following:

- whether or not the participants are used to meeting and discussing ideas
- how the members feel about speaking up in front of their leader and each other
- whether relations between participants are good or strained
- if there has been a recent layoff, personal tragedy or other event that might distract participants
- if members have well-developed group skills, such as listening, debating, decision making, etc.
- how the group has managed past meetings
- whether the leader or the organization is likely to support the ideas of the group

Creating the Conditions for Full Participation

As a facilitator you need to understand the basic pre-requisites for full participation. In general, people will participate fully if they

✎ ___ feel relaxed with the other participants
___ understand the topic under discussion
___ have had some say in the planning process
___ feel committed to the topic
___ have the information and knowledge needed for a fruitful discussion
___ feel 'safe' in expressing their opinions
___ aren't interfered with or otherwise unduly influenced
___ trust and have confidence in the facilitator
___ are comfortable and at ease in the meeting room
___ feel that the organization will support their ideas

A good rule is that the more resistant a group is likely to be, the more necessary it is to hold interviews or focus groups with members beforehand to get them involved and let them voice their concerns.

Removing the Blocks to Participation

Ensuring that people participate actively is one of your primary responsibilities. There is no excuse for running a meeting that a few people dominate or in which half the group sits in silent withdrawal. Here are some activities you can use to encourage active involvement:

Break the Ice

Even in a group where members know one another, they need to engage in ice breakers to set a warm and supportive tone.

Books on ice breakers abound. Do your homework so that you have at least four to six simple warm-up exercises handy at all times.

Clarify the Topic

At the start of any session, make sure everyone is clear about the purpose of the meeting by

    __ reviewing what created the need for the meeting so that everyone understands its history

    __ sharing the input members gave during any surveys, focus groups or interviews to demonstrate member participation in creating the goal

    __ asking all present to ratify the purpose statement to ensure full understanding and commitment

    __ stating the goal of the facilitation so everyone is clear about the desired outcome

Always be alert to the fact that even a crystal clear purpose can quickly become cloudy. Members can get sidetracked or suddenly decide there's a more important issue to be discussed.

It's quite common for facilitators to have to redefine the design of a session in midstream. (That's what makes facilitating such a challenge.) The wise facilitator is always open to making changes. Forcing a group to continue a discussion that no longer makes sense, just 'because it's on the agenda,' is a sure formula for disaster.

Create Buy-In

People are very cynical these days so it's especially important to check with your group to determine how many of the following harsh realities are going to be a factor:

___ people are working extra hours and don't know how they'll find the time to attend the session

___ facilitated meetings usually generate many action plans, which is extra work no one wants

___ the organization may not support the ideas generated by employees; priorities could shift tomorrow

___ a feeling that the improvements gained will only benefit the organization

An effective buy-in activity is to pair up participants at the start of any session and ask them to spend five minutes discussing two questions:

"What is the gain for the organization in solving this problem, fixing this process, etc.?"

"How will I personally benefit if we solve this problem, fix this process, etc.?"

After the partner discussion, participants can recount their own or their partner's responses. Record all comments on the flip charts. The participants' responses to question #2 amounts to their psychological buy-in to the session.

In cases of heightened levels of resistance, add two additional questions to the partner buy-in exercise:

"What's blocking me personally from participating? Why might I be reluctant?"

"What will it take to overcome these blocks? Under what conditions, and with what support, will I consider giving this my full attention?"

When you record members' responses to these two further questions, you'll, in effect, be negotiating their participation. Having their conditions on the table lets you assess the extent to which the participants are feeling blocked.

The problem with identifying the blocks is, of course, that you may not be in a position to negotiate many of these items. If you anticipate strong resistance, it's best to surface the blocks in the planning phase. This allows time to negotiate the support issues before the session. The results of the resistance negotiations can then be presented at the beginning of the session to help relieve concerns and help people move forward with commitment. In high-resistance situations, the manager, and even senior manager, may have to be present at the start of the meeting to respond to the concerns expressed by the members.

Remember to vary the buy-in question for different situations. To create 'buy-in' for a process-improvement exercise, ask group members the following:

> *"How will my work life be made easier if we manage to simplify this process?"*

To create 'buy-in' for joining a team, ask group members:

> *"What are the possible benefits for me, personally, if I become a member of this team?"*

To create 'buy-in' for learning a new skill, ask group members:

> *"How is learning to operate the new software going to benefit my career?"*

Make Eye Contact

This is a simple but a very important technique to improve participation. By looking directly at the more quiet people, you're telling them that they haven't been forgotten.

Help Participants Prepare

We all know what a colossal waste of time a meeting can be if no one is prepared and people are forced to make decisions without adequate information. To prevent this from happening at your session, make sure the purpose of the meeting is clear and communicate this information before the meeting so that people have time to get ready. If the meeting is expected to be complex, have a small group meet ahead of time to identify who needs to do which portion of the 'homework'. If the group is small, you might call each person to make sure they understand their 'homework' assignment.

When people do adequate pre-work, they gain confidence and will often participate much more actively.

Create Targeted Norms

All groups need guidelines to ensure a cooperative and supportive climate. Rules should be written by the participants themselves. Typical meeting norms could include: *being on time, respecting each other's opinions, listening actively, debating differences of opinion calmly, honoring privacy, being supportive rather than judgemental, taking responsibility for actions, etc.*

If there seems to be a significant amount of reluctance to speak up, the group can create specific, targeted norms to ensure that members feel safe enough to participate. 'Safety' norms are an example of targeted norms. In this case, norms are created for the comfort of participants who may feel that they're operating in a particularly sensitive environment.

Help members create safety norms by asking the following questions:

> *"What rules should we establish today that will ensure that no one feels they can't speak up with confidence? Under what conditions are you going to be able to freely speak your mind?"*

Some sample 'safety' norms include the following:

- all ideas are good and will be listened to carefully
- all discussions are strictly confidential (i.e. "what's said here, stays here")
- both people and issues will be handled with respect
- there will be no retaliation on the basis of anything that is said in this meeting
- no one will personally attack another person
- all feedback must be phrased in a constructive and supportive manner
- everyone will use neutral body language (i.e. "no pointing, shaking fingers, crossing arms, etc.")
- instead of just arguing our points, we'll listen to and acknowledge each other's ideas first
- anyone can call a timeout if they're confused about the topic or feel that the discussion is going off track or want a change in how a topic is being handled

Targeted norms may also be necessary in a range of other situations.

- If the group has experienced **conflict,** ask a norming question such as:

    "What rules do we need to set today to ensure we manage conflict at this meeting?"

- If any members of the group are reluctant to participate, ask:

    "What guidelines should we establish that will encourage participation and help all members feel their ideas are important?"

- If the group has trouble staying on track, ask this question:

    "What rules will help ensure that we stay on track and on time today?"

As with regular norms, targeted norms need to be developed by the participants, in response to specific situations. If there's no response when you ask the normative question, divide members into pairs or subgroups and ask the question again. Then, gather up their ideas.

Set Up the Room to Encourage Participation

How you arrange a room will greatly affect how group members interact. Theatre-style seating is the worst possible arrangement for facilitating an active discussion. People automatically assume that they'll be spoken at. It also discourages people from looking at each other.

Large boardroom tables have an especially stifling effect on people. This is very unfortunate since many large companies have huge boardroom tables struck squarely in the middle of their best meeting room. If either theatre-style seating or boardroom tables are your only option, break people into pairs, trios and foursomes as often as possible to keep everyone talking.

If you have any choice in the matter of seating, select a large room and try to get small, modular tables. Small rectangles arranged in a large horseshoe for whole group sessions or smaller squares for small group discussions are the best.

If the group has more than ten people, break it into

small groups of not more than six people per group. People can sit in their small groups, even when the whole group is in session. Small groups always help break the ice and create a more private forum for discussions.

High-Participation Techniques

There are many excellent techniques available to get even the most reluctant and shy participant to play an active part. These techniques offer anonymity to members and generate lots of activity.

Discussion Partners

This simple technique can be used as a way of starting any discussion. After posing a question to a large group, ask everyone to find a partner and discuss the question for a few minutes. Have people report on what they talked about. You can use this with threesomes as well.

Tossed Salad

Place an empty cardboard box or an inexpensive plastic salad bowl on the table. Give out small slips of paper and ask people to write down one good idea per slip. Have them toss the slips into the bowl. When people have finished writing, have someone 'toss the salad.' Pass around the bowl so that each person can take out as many slips as they tossed in. Go around the table and have people share ideas before discussing and refining the most promising ones together.

Issues and Answers

When faced with a long list of issues to tackle, rather

than attempting to problem solve all of them as a whole group (which would take forever), post the problems around the room. Put only one issue on each sheet of flip-chart paper.

Ask all members to go to one of the issue sheets and discuss that problem with whomever else was drawn to that sheet. Make sure people are distributed evenly, with at least three people per issue. You can use chairs, but this works best as a stand-up activity.

Allow up to five minutes for the subgroups to analyze the situation. Have them make notes on the top half of the flip-chart sheet. Ring a bell and ask everyone to move to another flip-chart sheet. When they get there, ask them to read the analysis made by the first group and to add any additional ideas. This round is often shorter than five minutes. Keep moving people around until everyone is back at their original sheet.

Once the analysis round is complete, ask everyone to return to the original issue they started with. Ask them to generate and record solutions to their respective issue on the bottom half of the sheet. Once again circulate people until everyone has added ideas on all of the sheets.

To end the process, have everyone walk by each sheet, read the solutions and check off the one or two ideas they think are the best.

When everyone is seated again, go through the ideas together and then ask the small groups to each take responsibility for creating action plans for the ideas on one of the sheets.

Talk Circuit

This technique works best in a large crowd because it creates a strong buzz and lets people get to know each other. Start by posing a question to the group and then allow quiet time for each person to write their own response.

Ask everyone to sit 'knee to knee' with a partner and share their ideas. Have one person speak while the other acts as facilitator. After two to three minutes ring a bell and have partners reverse their roles. After two or three more minutes stop the discussions.

Ask everyone to find a new partner and repeat the process, but in slightly less time. Stop the action and then have everyone repeat the process with a third partner.

In the final round allow only one minute per person. When the partner discussions are over, discuss the ideas as a whole group and record them on flip charts.

Pass the Envelope

Give each person an envelope filled with blank slips of paper. Pose a question or challenge to the group, and then have everyone write down as many ideas as they can within the given time frame and put the slips into the envelope. Tell people to pass the envelopes, either to the next person or in all directions, and when the passing stops, read the contents. Pair off participants and have them discuss the ideas in their two envelopes. What ideas did they receive? What are the positives and negatives of each idea? What other ideas should they add? Combine pairs to form groups of four and ask them to further refine the content of their four envelopes into practical action plans. Hold a plenary to collect ideas.

Use this survey if all members aren't participating fully. For conducting a Survey Feedback meeting see page 151.

 Group Effectiveness Survey

Instructions to Members:

Read over the following statements. Rate how your group manages the participation of its members. Be totally honest. Remember that this survey is anonymous. The results will be tabulated and fed back to the group members for their assessment.

1. Commitment — Member commitment to our goal is high

1	2	3	4	5
totally disagree	disagree somewhat	not sure	agree somewhat	totally disagree

2. Acceptance — Members are friendly, concerned and interested in each other

1	2	3	4	5
totally disagree	disagree somewhat	not sure	agree somewhat	totally disagree

3. Belonging — Members feel a close bond with each other

1	2	3	4	5
totally disagree	disagree somewhat	not sure	agree somewhat	totally disagree

4. Involvement — All members play an active role. The group isn't dominated by one or two strong individuals

1	2	3	4	5
totally disagree	disagree somewhat	not sure	agree somewhat	totally disagree

5. Support — Members listen to and respect each other's views

1	2	3	4	5
totally disagree	disagree somewhat	not sure	agree somewhat	totally disagree

6. Respect — Members appreciate each other's different strengths. Everyone is valued for their specific skills

1	2	3	4	5
totally disagree	disagree somewhat	not sure	agree somewhat	totally disagree

7. Tolerance — Members recognize and accept individual differences

1	2	3	4	5
totally disagree	disagree somewhat	not sure	agree somewhat	totally disagree

8. Recognition — Members give each other positive feedback about excellent performance

1	2	3	4	5
totally disagree	disagree somewhat	not sure	agree somewhat	totally disagree

Encouraging Effective Meeting Behaviors

Sometimes you'll find yourself working with unruly groups: people interrupt, members run in and out, people dismiss others' ideas prematurely, and so on.

Producing outcomes is a battle in these situations. The wisest thing to do is stop the proceedings and give the members a crash course in effective meeting behaviors:

1. Introduce the idea that certain behaviors are less effective than others. Hand out the sheets on the next two pages, which describe effective and ineffective meeting behaviors. Go over each behavior described. Answer any questions.

2. Appoint a group member to be the observer for the rest of the meeting. Give this person the observation sheet and ask them to note all occurrences of the listed behaviors, keeping track of the names of people and the specific thing they did or said. (The observer may need to sit on the sidelines, although some people are able to observe and also participate.)

3. At the end of the session, set aside some time to hear from the observer. Were there more effective or ineffective behaviors displayed? What were some specific examples of each type?

4. Ask members for their observations. At the end of this discussion, the group should be asked to write new norms by which to govern itself.

Group Behaviors Handout

In order to be effective when working together, we all need to be aware of individual and collective behaviors.

Behaviors That Help Effectiveness:

Behavior	Description
Listens Actively	looks at the person who is speaking, nods, asks probing questions and acknowledges what is said by paraphrasing point(s) made
Supports	encourages others to develop ideas and make suggestions; gives them recognition
Probes	goes beyond the surface comments by questioning teammates to uncover hidden information
Clarifies	asks members for more information about what they mean; clears up confusion
Offers Ideas	shares suggestions, ideas, solutions and proposals
Includes Others	asks quiet members for their opinion, making sure no one is left out
Summarizes	pulls together ideas from a number of people; determines where the group is at and what has been covered
Harmonizes	reconciles opposing points of view; links together similar ideas; points out where ideas are the same
Manages Conflict	listens to the views of others; clarifies issues and key points made by opponents; seeks solutions

Behaviors That Hinder Effectiveness:

Behavior	Description
Yeah But's'	discredits the ideas of others
Blocks	insists on getting one's way; doesn't compromise; stands in the way of the team's progress
Grandstands	draws attention to one's personal skills; boasts
Goes Off Topic	directs the conversation onto other topics
Dominates	tries to "run" the group through dictating and/or bullying
Withdraws	doesn't participate or offer help or support to others
Devil's Advocate	takes pride in being contrary
Criticizes	makes negative comments about people or their ideas
Personal Slurs	hurls insults at other people

Chapter 5
Facilitating Conflict

*D*ealing with conflict is a fact of every facilitator's life. Accepting conflict is inevitable, and being prepared to deal with it will only work to your advantage!

Debates vs. Arguments

Understanding the differences between debates and arguments is critical. Healthy debate is essential – a group that doesn't express differences of opinion is incapable of making effective decisions. Dysfunctional arguments, however, lead to disaster!

In Healthy Debates	In Dysfunctional Arguments
people are open to hearing other's ideas	people assume they're right
people listen and respond to ideas even if they don't agree with them	people wait until others have finished talking, then state their ideas without responding to ideas of the other person
everyone tries to understand the views of the other person	no one is interested in how the other person sees the situation
people stay objective and focus on the facts	people get personally attacked and blamed
there's a systematic approach to analyzing the situation and looking for solutions	hot topics get thrashed out in an unstructured way

Techniques that Create Healthy Debate	Techniques that Allow Dysfunctional Arguments
→ stay totally neutral	→ join the argument
→ point out differences so they can be understood	→ ignore differences – just pray they will go away
→ insist that people listen	→ let people be rude – set no norms
→ have rules - use them politely	→ ignore the fact that no one is really hearing anyone else
→ make people paraphrase each other's ideas	→ side step hot issues
→ ask for concerns	→ let people get personal
→ make people focus on facts	→ get defensive
→ problem solve concerns	→ squash dissent
→ invite and face feedback	→ stand by passively
→ facilitate assertively	→ let it drag
→ get closure and move on	

Steps in Managing Conflict - Overview

Facilitating conflict has two distinct steps:

Step 1: Venting

This involves listening to people so they feel that they are heard and any built-up emotions are diffused. People are rarely ready to move on to solutions until their emotional blocks have been removed.

Step 2: Resolving the issue

This step involves choosing the right structured approach to get solutions. The approach can be collaborative, problem solving, compromising, accommodating or consciously avoiding.

Let's look at each step in more detail.

Step 1: Venting Emotions

Not every difference of opinion is characterized by intense emotions. There are groups who objectively surface issues, calmly discuss the facts, listen politely to each other and collaborate to find the best solution.

Unfortunately, you won't encounter them often enough. More often, facilitators see any of the following behaviors in conflict situations:

- people pushing their point of view, without being at all receptive to the ideas of others
- people becoming angry, defensive and personal with each other
- negative body language, like glaring and finger pointing
- sarcastic or dismissive remarks
- people 'yeah butting' and criticizing each other's ideas
- quiet people 'shutting down' to stay out of it
- extreme anger to the point where relationships are damaged

It's the facilitator's job to properly handle negative emotions as soon as they emerge, so that they don't poison the dynamics of the group. When people start to get emotional there are some basic strategies that the facilitator should employ:

Slow things down – Get the attention of the group by stopping the action and asking people to slow down. You can use the excuse that you can't take notes as quickly as people are talking. Ask them to start over and repeat key ideas.

Stay totally neutral – Never take sides or allow your body language to hint that you favor one idea or one person over another.

Stay calm – Maintain your composure and do not raise your own voice. Speak slowly with an even tone. Avoid emotional body language.

Revisit the norms – Point out the existing norms and remind people that they agreed to them earlier on. Engage the group in writing new norms.

Be assertive – Move into the referee mode. Insist that people speak one at a time. Make them put their hands up and stop people who interrupt others. Don't stand by passively while people fight.

Raise Awareness – On a clean sheet of flip-chart paper record member ideas about the difference between a debate versus an argument. Ask them which one they want to have.

Make interventions – Don't let people fight with each other or display rudeness. Refer to pg. 66 in this chapter for the appropriate wording for different interventions.

Emphasize listening – Paraphrase key points and ask others to do the same thing. Hand out, discuss, and then enforce the practices outlined on pg. 54.

Call time out – Don't hesitate to stop the action any time emotions get out of hand or if the discussion is spinning in circles. Ask: *"Are we making progress? Are we using the right approach? How are people feeling?"* Act on their suggestions for improving the meeting. Refer to pg. 28 on process checking for more on how to handle timeouts.

Use a structured approach – Use techniques such as Forcefield Analysis, Multi-voting, Systematic Problem Solving, Cause and Effect Analysis, etc. Don't let a discussion rage on without imposing structure and systematically capturing key ideas. Chapter 8 provides detailed descriptions of the most commonly used facilitator tools.

Use the flip chart – Make notes of key points so they aren't lost and the group members don't have to go over the whole thing again. Read back the notes on the flip chart whenever you want to regain control for a few minutes.

Create closure – Make sure that the debating is really going somewhere. Ask group members to help summarize what has been agreed to. Test these items for agreement. Help the group create action plans to ensure implementation of key suggestions.

Step 2: Resolving Issues

Here are five basic approaches you can choose from once emotions have been vented, in order to resolve the underlying issue:

Avoid:	Ignore the conflict in the hope that it will go away. Maintain silence or try to change the subject.

....

Accommodate: Ask people to be more tolerant and accept each other's views. Ask them to try getting along. This sometimes involves asking one person to give in to another person.

Compromise: Look for the middle ground between highly polarized views. Ask each person to give up some of what he/she wants in order to get other items he/she thinks are more important.

Compete: Use force to make points and quell any conflicts. Go for a personal win even if the other person feels like he/she has lost the argument.

Collaborate: Face the conflict, draw people's attention to it, surface the issues and resolve them in a win/win way by using systematic problem solving.

....

Using the Conflict Management Approaches

<u>Avoiding</u> doesn't deal with the issue	→ Use it in those 10% of situations when issues can't be resolved profitably
<u>Accommodating</u> just smoothes things over	→ Use it only in those 5% of situations where keeping the peace is of more importance than finding a solution
<u>Competing</u> divides groups and creates win/lose	→ Facilitators should never compete! Zero percent applicability
<u>Compromising</u> helps find the middle ground	→ Use it in those 20% of situations when faced with polarized choices
<u>Collaborating</u> helps get people working together to find the best solution for everyone	→ This is the #1 preferred approach for all facilitators. Use it in 65% of all conflict situations

Collaboration encourages people to work together to objectively seek solutions that they can all live with. Because it's consensual, it unites and generates solutions that everyone feels committed to implementing. It is the superior conflict option!

Assumptions underlying collaboration

Collaboration is a superior way of solving a problem during a meeting; however, a number of conditions need to be in place to ensure a successful outcome.

Members must share the following:

   __ have sufficient trust among themselves to open up and be supportive of each other when necessary

   __ have a positive intent to work towards a win/win solution

   __ have relevant information on hand to make a sound decision

   __ have the time to make this decision

   __ believe the topic is important enough to warrant spending the time it will take

Making Interventions

During any workshop or meeting, there are many occasions when the facilitator will need to make an intervention. The definition of 'intervention' is, "any action or set of actions deliberately taken to improve the functioning of the group." This may be necessary in the following situations:

* someone isn't listening
* two people are having a side conversation
* people are interrupting each other
* one person uses a sarcastic tone during a debate
* people's comments get personal
* the discussion is getting off track

Intervening is like holding up a mirror to the participants so that they can see what they're doing and take steps to correct the problem.

The need to intervene may arise because of one individual, or it may be interpersonal, involving a conflict between two or more people.

Problems that arise could range from poor listening to using the wrong process. (i.e. using a Forcefield Analysis instead of Cause and Effect Analysis).

You always need to be cautious about whether or not to intervene. If you intervened every single time there was a problem, you might be interrupting too frequently. Instead, you need to keep a watchful eye for repetitive, inappropriate behaviors that don't seem to resolve themselves.

Deciding Whether or Not to Intervene

Below is a set of questions to ask when deciding if an intervention is advisable.

• Is the problem serious?
• Might it go away by itself?
• How much time will intervening take? Do we have that time?
• How much of a disruption will intervening cause?
• How will it impact relationships; the flow of the meeting?
• Can the intervention hurt the climate?
• Will it damage anyone's self-esteem?
• What's the chance that the intervention will work?
• Do I know these people well enough to do this?
• Do I have enough credibility to do this?
• Is it appropriate to intervene given their level of openness and trust?

Finally, a good question to ask yourself is, *"What will happen if I do nothing?"* If the answer is that the group will be less effective if you do nothing, you're obligated to take action.

Wording Interventions

Interventions are always risky since they can make the situation worse. For this reason, interventions need to be worded carefully. There are generally three distinct components to an intervention statement:

Step 1: **Describe what you're seeing**. This is non-judgmental and doesn't attribute motive. It is based solely on observations of actual events. e.g. *"Allen and Sue, both of you have left and returned three times during this meeting"*

Step 2: **Make an impact statement.** Tell members how their actions are impacting on you, the process, or other people. Base this on actual observations. e.g. *"We had to stop our discussions and start over again on three occasions because of your comings and goings over the last hour. I'm feeling extremely frustrated and I'm sensing that I'm not alone."*

Step 3: **Redirect the person's behavior(s).** This can be done in the following ways: (a) asking members for their suggestions about what to do (i.e. *"What can you do to make sure this doesn't happen again?"*)

(b) telling members what to do (e.g. *"Please either leave or stay for the rest of the meeting."*)

Special Note: *Impact statements (Step 2 above) can be omitted from an intervention if they are interpreted as laying excessive guilt on the offending parties. You need to use your judgment as to whether or not the situation requires a focus on 'impact.' A good rule of thumb is to use impact statements when the offensive behavior is persistent or repetitive and previous intervention attempts have been ignored.*

Intervention Wording for Specific Situations

When people start to get emotional, there are specific responses that can effectively redirect negative behavior in different situations. You will notice that none of these redirecting statements put down the person or is in any way critical. All of them offer the other person a chance to save face and to say or do the right thing next time.

When someone is being sarcastic:

> *"Ellen, I'm afraid your good ideas aren't being heard because of the tone of voice you're using. How about stating that again, only in a more neutral way?"*

When one person is putting down the ideas of another:

> *"Joe, you have been 'yes butting' every suggestion Carol has put on the table. I'm going to ask you to explore these ideas by asking a few questions to make sure you fully understand them before*

dismissing them. It will make Carol feel more like she's being heard."

When two people are arguing, cutting each other off and not listening to each other:

"I'm afraid neither of you are hearing the excellent points being made by the other. I'm going to ask you both to first paraphrase what the other has said before you make your own comment."

When someone is inappropriately aggressive or hurtful to another person:

"Fred, I'm going to stop you from saying anything further for just a moment and ask June to tell you how she would like to have you interact with her during the rest of this meeting. June, what would be better than this?"

When one person dominates the discussion:

"Al, you always have lots of valuable ideas, but we need to hear from the other members of the team. Would you please hold your comments until the end so that other people can be heard."

When someone has hurled a personal slur at someone else:

"Jim, rather than characterizing Sally as being 'sloppy,' please tell her specifically about the state of the meeting room after her session, so that she can address the situation."

When two people are trashing each other's ideas without giving them a fair hearing:

> "You are discounting each other's ideas very
> quickly. I'm going to ask that you give a quick
> recap of what the other person said before
> launching into your points."

When a person makes only negative remarks about the ideas of another person:

> "Mary, what do you like about what Chuck just
> said?"

When people run in and out of a meeting:

> "In the last ten minutes, three people have gone
> in and out of this meeting, disrupting the discus-
> sion. What ought to be done about this?"

When everyone has fallen silent:

> "Everyone has become pretty quiet in the last few
> minutes and we haven't had any new ideas.
> What can we do to get things going again?"

When the whole group is acting dysfunctional:

> "I'm going to stop this discussion. I'm noticing
> that two people are talking among themselves
> while three others are arguing emotionally. What
> can we do to make the rest of this meeting run
> more smoothly?"

Members are disregarding their previously set norms:

> "I'm going to suggest we stop this meeting for a
> few minutes to look back at the norms we set
> last week. Are we following them? Do we need
> to add a few new ones?"

When the meeting has totally digressed:

> "I need to point out that we have now digressed
> and are onto another topic. Is this the topic the
> team wants to discuss or should we park it and
> go back to the original agenda item?"

Telling Versus Asking

In some of the preceding interventions, the facilitator told people what to do, while in others they were asked. Still in others, it sounded like the facilitator was only making a suggestion.

When you're making an intervention you need to make a judgment about which of these approaches to use, situation by situation. While there are no hard and fast rules, here are some principles:

- asking is always better than telling because people are more likely to accept their own intervention
- it's always appropriate for facilitators to suggest or tell people what to do on matters of process
- a directive or telling response is appropriate if the individuals are exhibiting extremely dysfunctional behavior
- the more a group acts maturely and responsible, the more effective it is to ask, rather than tell

Dealing With Resistance

As a facilitator, you always need to have a strategy ready for dealing with situations in which a group resists. Groups can resist your facilitation efforts for a number of reasons:

- the timing or location of the meeting might be poor
- the topic of the meeting may not reflect their needs
- they may have received insufficient notice of the meeting
- they're afraid of taking on a new task that entails taking risks
- they suspect that nothing will happen as a result of the meeting
- they feel that the organization isn't behind them, etc.

Sometimes this resistance comes out into the open when an outspoken member gets up and vents concern. At other times it remains hidden, only expressed in people's negative body language or lack of participation.

When you encounter resistance there's a right and a wrong way to deal with it. Using the wrong way will make the resistance grow. Choosing the right approach will make it manageable.

The Right Approach for Dealing with Resistance

The right approach for handling resistance always consists of two steps:

Step 1: Invite the resistor to express his or her resistance while you listen actively, paraphrase and offer empathy.

"Tell me why you feel this way?"

"What happened last time?"

"What are all of the things that are making you resist?"

Step 2: After all the concerns have been acknowledged, ask questions to prompt the resistor to suggest solutions to the barriers.

"What circumstances would make you willing to stay?"

"What assurance will eliminate your concerns?"

"What supports will enable you to continue?"

Common Facilitation Dilemmas

Regardless of how well a session is prepared, there are always things that can go wrong. The following are common facilitation dilemmas and strategies that can help.

Scenario #1: The group resists being facilitated

The group desperately needs structure for its discussions, but doesn't like following a step-by-step process. They insist they don't want a facilitator. Members say it feels too formal. Sometimes there's a controlling chairperson present and he or she rejects the idea of having a formal facilitator.

Strategy: Facilitate from your seat at the side of the table. At appropriate moments, offer the group methods for tackling parts of the discussion. Informally act as timekeeper. Facilitate the discussion innocuously: ask questions, paraphrase, synthesize ideas and include quiet people, just as if you were up at the front of the room. Make notes on regular paper and offer your summaries when they're appropriate.

Potential facilitator mistake: Accepting that the group doesn't want process help and letting them flounder. While it's always best to be able to "officially" facilitate, it's possible to help a group by covertly playing the process role. Some attention to process is better than none.

Scenario #2: Early in the meeting it appears the original agenda is wrong

In spite of data gathering and proper planning it becomes clear that the entire premise for the meeting is wrong. The group legitimately needs to discuss something else.

Strategy: Stop the meeting and verify your assessment that the existing agenda is now redundant. Take time to do agenda building. Ask members what they want to achieve at this session. Prioritize the issues and assign times. Take a fifteen minute break to regroup and create a new process design. Ratify the new agenda with the members. Be flexible and stay focused on the needs of the group.

Potential facilitator mistake: Forcing the group to follow the original agenda because of the energy and preparation that went into creating the design.

Scenario #3: The meeting goes hopelessly off-track

Members are usually good at staying focused but have now gone totally off-track and refuse to return to the planned agenda.

Strategy: Stop the off topic discussion and determine if members are aware that they're off topic and if they're comfortable with this. If they decide they want to stay with this new topic, help them structure their discussion. Ask:

> "How long do you want to devote to this? What's the goal of this new discussion? What tools or methods should we use?, etc."

You should then facilitate the new discussion. If at any point they decide to return to the original agenda, 'park' the current discussion and return to it at the end of the meeting to determine what should be done with it.

Potential facilitator mistake: Stepping down from the facilitator role because the group isn't following the planned agenda, or allowing the group to have a lengthy off-topic discussion in an unstructured manner. Trying to force the group back on topic when members feel a pressing need to discuss something else creates unnecessary conflict.

Scenario #4: Group members ignore the process they originally agreed on

There is a clear process for the session, but the members simply ignore it. When you attempt to get people to follow the agreed method, they revert to random discussion.

Strategy: Let them go on this way for a while, then ask the following questions:

> "How's this going? Are we getting anywhere?"

Once a group has recognized that it isn't making progress, members are often ready to accept a more structured approach.

Potential facilitator mistake: Giving up and ceasing to watch for an opening to step back in and offer structure. Taking an 'I told you so' attitude if members admit frustration with their approach.

Scenario #5: The group ignores its own norms

Members have set clear behavioral norms, but start acting in ways that break all of their own rules.

Strategy: Allow them to be dysfunctional for a while, then ask the following:

> *"How do you feel this meeting is going in terms of the rules we set?"*
>
> *"Why do you think it's so hard sticking to the rules?"*
>
> *"How can we make sure we follow the rules?"*

Implement member suggestions. If they don't suggest anything, recommend that one or two group members be in charge of calling the group's attention to the rules any time they're being ignored or broken. This puts the onus on members to police themselves.

Potential facilitator mistake: Making all the interventions yourself and failing to use peer pressure to manage behavior.

Scenario #6: People use the session to unload emotional baggage

The agenda is swept off the table as people start venting their frustrations about their job, other people or the organization.

Strategy: Often groups can't focus on the task at hand because of pent-up feelings that have not been dealt with or recognized. In these cases it's healthy to encourage participants to release feelings by getting them out into the open. The key is to structure the venting so that it can be managed and the feelings can be channeled into appropriate actions.

Some useful questions for managing venting sessions include the following:

> "How important is it that we share these feelings now?"
>
> "Do we need to have any rules (safety norms) about how we do this?"
>
> "How long do we do it?"
>
> "Are any of these issues problems we can solve?"
>
> "What can we do to solve these problems?"

Potential facilitator mistake: Trying to suppress the venting process or letting it happen without any structure.

Scenario #7: No matter what techniques are used, no decision is reached

The group has been discussing options for hours and no clear decision is emerging. The discussion is spinning in circles and precious time is being wasted.

Strategy: Stop the action and look at the decision method that is being used. There are many decisions that simply cannot be made through consensus or voting. Consider using another method like a decision grid (see pg. 146) that allows for a comparative rating of individual aspects of competing options.

Another approach is to analyze the blocks to making a final decision. Ask this question:

> *"What are all the things that are keeping us
> from making a decision?"*

List these and spend some time removing these decision barriers.

Potential facilitator mistake: Letting the group
spin around for the entire meeting without checking the
decision method and/or examining the decision barriers.

Scenario #8: Members refuse to report back their discussions

After a small group discussion, no one is willing to
come forward and present the group's ideas back to the
larger group. There's a real concern that one or several
of the ideas are too sensitive and that there might be
repercussions.

Strategies: Divide the presentation and have two to
three members from each group share the spotlight. If
there's much material, the whole team can present portions back to the larger group. Also set the stage with
the larger group by asking them to listen with an open
mind and not react negatively to the presentation before
having explored its potential.

Potential facilitator mistake: Taking the burden
from the members and speaking for them. This shifts
responsibility for the recommendations from members
to yourself, and can result in members taking little
responsibility for follow-up actions.

Scenario #9: Members balk at assuming any responsibility for action plans

People love discussing problems and brainstorming

ideas, but when it comes to action planning, everyone is suddenly too busy or insecure about their ability to complete the task.

Strategy: Ensure that it's clear from the start that any problem-solving exercise includes action planning and that members will be expected to assume major responsibility for implementing their ideas.

Implementing action plans is often a growth activity if people can be given support and encouragement to stretch beyond their present capabilities. When people are concerned that they can't succeed, ask them the following:

> "What help, training, and/or other supports do you need?"

Work to provide those enabling resources.

If members have time barriers to participating in implementation, these need to be identified and problem solved. Organizations often ask the same hardworking people to be on every committee. If there's any control over who is going to be asked to work on an activity, considerable thought should be given to whether these individuals have the time needed to devote to the activity.

Potential facilitator mistake: Letting people 'off the hook' too easily by not problem solving the blocks or letting the same people shoulder all of the work. The worst strategy of all is to take responsibility for the action steps yourself.

Use the following sheet when you wish to provide detailed feedback to two people interacting during conflict.

✎ Observing Interpersonal Conflict Worksheet

Behaviors that help	Person "A"	Person "B"
1. Leaning forward – listening actively		
2. Paraphrasing – "Is this what you're saying?"		
3. Questioning to clarify – "Let me understand this better."		
4. Showing respect for the other's opinion – valuing input		
5. Calmness – voice tone low, relaxed body posture		
6. Open and vulnerable – showing flexibility		
7. Clearly stating my position – assertive stance		
8. Checking for agreement on what is to be resolved		
9. Laying out ground rules – "What will help us?"		
10. Showing empathy – perception checking		
11. "I" statements – disclosing feelings		
12. Using other person's name		
13. Body contact – if appropriate		
14. Problem solving – looking at alternatives		
15. Win/Win attitude – concern for other person		
16. Congruence – between verbal & nonverbal behavior		
17. Concern for other person's goal		
18. Feedback – giving specific descriptive details		

Observing Interpersonal Conflict Worksheet

Behaviors that hinder	Person "A"	Person "B"
1. Interrupting		
2. Showing disrespect		
3. Entrapment questions		
4. Talks too much		
5. Pushing for solution		
6. Arguing about personal perception		
7. Aggressive manner		
8. Accusing, laying blame		
9. Smirking, getting personal		
10. "You made me" statements		
11. Non-receptive to suggestions		
12. Not identifying real feelings		
13. Ending before finishing		
14. Incongruity of words and actions		
15. Defensiveness		
16. Denying, not owning problems		
17. Blocking, talking off topic – changing the subject		
18. Not giving specific feedback		

Use this observation sheet when you want to give feedback to a group about how they handled conflict.

Group Conflict Checklist

	Comments
No plan or process for approaching the task Group wanders from one topic to another because there's no format for discussion. No time is taken at the start of the meeting to set up parameters.	
Lack of active listening Instead of acknowledging each other's points before making their own, each person pushes their own ideas in a totally unconnected sequence.	
Lack of closure The group moves from one topic to another without discussing the merits of previous ideas.	
Personal attacks People use a sarcastic tone, ignore each other, interrupt or even attack each other. They don't focus on the facts.	
No process checking The group forges ahead without ever stopping to discuss whether the process is working or requires modification.	
Dominant members A few people do all the talking. No one notices or even cares that some people are left out.	

✎ Group Conflict Checklist

	Comments

Poor time management
     Time isn't budgeted or monitored.
     Time is wasted on the wrong things.	

Folding
     People just give in when things get
     rough. They don't systematically follow
     issues through.	

Lack of skill
     Members don't possess any tools for
     making decisions. They also lack important
     interpersonal skills.	

Passive or nonexistent facilitation
     No one is providing order or policing the
     action. No notes are kept. Everyone is
     taking sides. If there's a facilitator, he or she
     is unwilling to assert him/herself to offer
     procedural options or keep order.	

If you want to help a team in conflict understand exactly what's going on, use this survey to surface specific problems. (Refer to pg. 151 for the details of managing survey feedback.)

✎ Conflict Effectiveness Survey

Read over the following statements and rate how your group currently manages conflict. Be totally honest. Remember that this survey is anonymous. The results will be tabulated and results will be fed back to the group for their assessment.

1. Listening

1	2	3	4	5	6	7

People assume
they're right

People are open to
hearing new ideas

2. Acknowledging

1	2	3	4	5	6	7

People put their ideas
on the table without acknowledging the points made by
others

People acknowledge
eachother's ideas even
when they don't agree
with them

3. Objectivity

1	2	3	4	5	6	7

We tend to get
emotional and argue for
our favorite ideas

We tend to stay calm
and look objectively
at the facts

4. Building

1	2	3	4	5	6	7

We tend not to admit
that anyone else's ideas
are good

We generally take the
ideas of fellow members
and try to build on them

5. Norms

1	2	3	4	5	6	7

We don't have or use
norms to manage
conflict situations

We have created a good
set of norms that work well
to help us manage conflicts

6. Trust and Openness

1	2	3	4	5	6	7

People don't say what is
really on their minds

There is a lot of trust
that you can say whatever
you have on your mind

7. Approach to Conflict

1	2	3	4	5	6	7

Most often we either
avoid or argue vehemently

We tend to collaborate
to find solutions we
can all live with

8. Interpersonal Behaviors

1	2	3	4	5	6	7

People often get emotional
and make personal attacks

We stay calm and stick to
the facts. No one ever gets
personally attacked

9. Structure

1	2	3	4	5	6	7

We never take a systematic
approach. Mostly we just
thrash out differences

There is always a clearly
defined process for analyzing
the situatuin and looking
for solutions

10. Closure

1	2	3	4	5	6	7

Most of our conflict sessions
end without resolution

We are excellent at getting
to solutions and clear
actions steps

11. Process Checking

1	2	3	4	5	6	7

Once an argument starts
we never call timeout and
correct ourselves

We always stop and take
a look at how we are
managing our conflicts so
we can improve

12. Time Management

1	2	3	4	5	6	7

When things get heated we
lose all track of time and
our agenda goes out the
window

We very carefully monitor
our time to make sure we
aren't wasting it, especially
when we get into conflict

13. Aftermath

1	2	3	4	5	6	7

People are usually angry
for a long timeafterward

We work at clearing
the air of hurt feelings

Chapter 6
Effective Decision-Making

*H*elping groups make high-quality decisions is the most important function of a facilitator. Unfortunately, decision making is also one of the most difficult things to do properly.

First, attune yourself to some typical scenarios that illustrate a poor decision process:

- Several members of the group have tuned out as the discussion enters its second half hour of floating aimlessly, with no resolution in sight
- When the big decision finally comes to the table there is little time left in the meeting, so there's only a brief discussion of the key points, followed by a show of hands to arrive at an agreement
- Two of the team's members have little to say during a lengthy discussion, but later complain to teammates about not being asked their opinions
- After an hour of talking no real decision has been reached, so discussion moves on to another topic
- Instead of debating ideas the discussion seems more like a clash of wills, as members battle it out to see who can win over the others
- Even though they hold strong views, people start to

fold or give in just to get it over with

- After the meeting is over several people are overheard complaining that they can't really support the decision that was made

If any of these sound familiar, you may be working with a group that needs to learn to become more effective decision makers.

Symptoms, Causes and Cures of Poor Decisions

When groups make poor-quality decisions, one or more of the following symptoms are likely taking place:

Symptom 1:   Aimless drifting and random discussions.

The same topic gets kicked around meeting after meeting without resolution. Feels like the group is spinning its wheels.

Cause: No plan or process for approaching the decision.

Group members simply launch into the discussion without any thought to which tools to use. Without a systematic approach, people start proposing solutions before there has been a thorough analysis of the situation. There is a lack of proper information. Everyone puts their favorite solution on the table. No one takes notes. No solution is ever definitively agreed to. Detailed action plans aren't written down.

Cure: The group needs a structured approach to decision making that uses the right decision making tool and is assertively facilitated.

<u>Symptom 2:</u> **The group uses voting on important items where total buy-in is important, then uses consensus to decide trivial issues.**

Cause: A lack of understanding decision making options.

The group does not understand what the six key decision-making tools are, and when to use them.

Cure: The group needs to be familiar with the six main decision-making options and consciously decide which to use before launching into any decision-making discussion. (Refer to pgs. 91-96.)

<u>Symptom 3:</u> **The group always seems to run out of time just when the important decisions get onto the table.**

Cause: Poor time management.

Time isn't budgeted or monitored. There is no detailed agenda that sets aside the time needed to deal with important items. Hence, time is wasted discussing unimportant items. Meetings often start/run late.

Cure: The group needs to create a detailed agenda before each meeting. At the meeting the facilitator needs to be assertive about staying on track and on time.

<u>Symptom 4:</u> **When an important item is on the table people get heated and argumentative. No one really listens to the opposing viewpoints. Everyone just pushes their point and tries to be right. Some**

members dominate, unconcerned that others are silent.

Cause: Poorly developed group interaction skills

No one is really listening to each other's points, just pushing their own. No one knows how to structure a decision-making session. Facilitation is nonexistent or weak. As a result there's an absence of the synergy you get when people build on each other's ideas. This confrontational style strains relationships, which only makes things worse.

Cure: The members need training in group effectiveness skills so that they can exhibit more listening, supporting and idea building. This can be through a formal team training session or through informal practice sessions interjected into their meetings. A training plan to teach members to be effective is included on pg. 53.

Symptom 5: **After a lengthy discussion, it becomes clear that every one is operating on slightly different assumptions about what the problem is and what the constraints or possibilities are.**

Cause: Failure to check assumptions

Everyone has a different view of the situation, and is basing their input on that view. Assumptions are never put on the table for sharing or testing.

Cure: Use probing questions up front, to uncover the assumptions underlying the statements made by members. These questions can be related to the situation, the organization or the people involved. Once the assumptions are on the table they can be tested and validated or eliminated. Members will then be operating within the same framework.

Symptom 6: **In spite of the fact that the discussion has been going in circles for some time, no one takes action to get things back on track.**

Cause: No process checking

Even when things are going nowhere and frustration levels are running high, no one knows to call time-out to take stock and regroup. This situation, once again, reflects the absence of facilitation.

Cure: Stop the discussion periodically to ask how things are going: if the pace is right, if people feel progress is being made, if people feel the right approach is being taken (refer to the discussion of process checking on pg. 28).

Decision-Making Survey

If you want to assess your group's current decision-making effectiveness, use the following checklist as a post-meeting survey or an observation sheet during a decision-making session. Feed back the data collected once the survey results have been tabulated.

1	2	3	4	5
Clear step-by-step process used				Lack of systematic planned approach

1	2	3	4	5
Thorough checking of assumptions				No checking of assumptions

1	2	3	4	5
Use of the right decision method				Overuse voting, misuse consensus

1	2	3	4	5
Active listening by members				No one builds on the ideas of others

1	2	3	4	5
People build on each other's ideas				People focus on their own ideas

1	2	3	4	5
Objectively debate ideas				Emotionally argue points of view

1	2	3	4	5
Periodic process checking				Never stopping to check

1	2	3	4	5
Time carefully managed				Use of time isn't planned

1	2	3	4	5
Active and assertive facilitation				Passive or lack of facilitation

1	2	3	4	5
Full and equal participation				Some dominate, others are passive

1	2	3	4	5
True closure				Little gets decided

1	2	3	4	5
Clear action plans				No plans to implement

The Six Decision-Making Options

As a facilitator you have six distinct decision-making methods available. Each of these options represents a different approach. Each has pros and cons associated with it. The decision option should always be chosen carefully to be sure it's the most appropriate method. These six options are as follows (in reverse order of their relative value):

Option 6: Spontaneous Agreement

This happens occasionally when there's a solution that is favored by everyone and 100% agreement seems to happen automatically. Unanimous decisions are usually made quickly. They are fairly rare and often occur in connection with the more trivial or simple issues.

Pros: It's fast, easy, everyone is happy, it unites the group.

Cons: May be too fast; perhaps the issue actually

needed discussion.

Uses: When lack of discussion isn't vital (i.e. issues are trivial); or when issues are not complex, requiring no in-depth discussion.

Option 5: One person decides

This is a decision that the group decides to refer to one person to make on behalf of the group. A common misconception among teams is that every decision needs to be made by the whole group. In fact, a one-person decision is often a faster and more efficient way to get resolution. The quality of any one person's decision can be raised considerably if the person making the decision gets advice and input from other group members before they decide.

Pros: It's fast and accountability is clear.

Cons: It can divide the group if the person deciding doesn't consult, or makes a decision that others can't live with. A one-person decision typically lacks both the buy-in and the synergy that comes from a group decision-making process.

Uses: When the issue is unimportant or small, when there's a clear expert in the group, when only one person has the information needed to make the decision and can't share it or when one person is solely accountable for the outcome.

Option 4: Compromise

A negotiated approach applicable when there are several distinct options and members are strongly polarized (neither side is willing to accept the solution/position put forth by the other side). A middle position is then created that incorporates ideas from both sides. Throughout the process of negotiation everyone wins a few of their favorite points, but also loses a few items they liked. The outcome is, therefore, something that no one is totally satisfied with. In compromises no one feels they got what they originally wanted, so the emotional reaction is often, "It's not really what I wanted but I'm going to have to live with it."

Pros: It generates lots of discussion and does create a solution.

Cons: Negotiating when people are pushing a favored point of view tends to be adversarial, hence this approach divides the group. In the end everyone wins, but everyone also loses.

Uses: When two opposing solutions are proposed, neither of which are acceptable to everyone; or when the group is strongly polarized and compromise is the only alternative.

Option 3: Multi-voting

This is a priority-setting tool that is useful in making decisions when the group has a lengthy set of options before them, and rank ordering the options, based on a set of criteria, will clarify the best course of action. (Refer to pg. 141).

Pros: It's systematic, objective, democratic, non-competitive, and participative. Everyone wins somewhat and feelings of loss are minimal. It's a fast way of sorting out a complex set of options.

Cons: It's often associated with limited discussion, hence, limited understanding of the options. This may force unsatisfactory choices on people, because the real priorities do not rise to the surface, or people are swayed by each other if the voting is done out in the open rather than electronically or by ballot.

Uses: When there's a long list of alternatives or items from which to choose or when choosing a set of criteria to identify the best course of action.

Option 2: Majority Voting

This involves asking people to choose the option they favor, once clear choices have been identified. Usual methods are a show of hands or secret ballot. The quality of voting is always enhanced if there's good discussion to share ideas before the vote is taken.

Pros: It's fast – decisions can be of high quality if a vote is preceded by a thorough analysis.

Cons: It can be too fast and low in quality if people vote based on their personal feelings without the benefit of hearing each other's thoughts or facts. It creates winners and losers, hence dividing the group. The show of hands method may put pressure on people to conform.

Uses: When there are two distinct options and one or the other must be chosen; when decisions must be made quickly, and a division in the group is acceptable; when consensus has been attempted and can't be reached.

Option 1: Consensus Building

Involves everyone clearly understanding the situation or problem to be decided, analyzing all of the relevant facts together and then jointly developing solutions that represent the whole group's best thinking about the optimal decision. It's characterized by a lot of listening, healthy debate and testing of options. Consensus generates a decision about which everyone says, "I can live with it."

Pros: It's a collaborative effort that unites the group. It demands high involvement. It's systematic, objective and fact-driven. It builds buy-in and high commitment to the outcome.

Cons: It's time consuming and produces low-quality decisions if done without proper data collection or if members have poor interpersonal skills.

Uses: When decisions will impact the entire group; when buy-in and ideas from all members are essential; when the importance of the decision being made is worth the time it will take to complete the consensus process properly.

> *Remember that each option has its place so choose the most appropriate method before each decision-making session.*

Decision Options Chart

Option	Pros	Cons	Uses
Spontaneous Agreement	• fast, easy • unites	• too fast • lack of discussion	• when full discussion isn't critical • trivial issues
One Person	• can be fast • clear accountability	• lack of input • low buy-in • no synergy	• when one person is the expert • individual willing to take sole responsibility
Compromise	• discussion creates a solution	• adversarial win/lose • divides the group	• when positions are polarized; consensus improbable
Multi-Voting	• systematic • objective • participative • feels like a win	• limits dialogue • influenced choices • real priorities may not surface	• to sort or prioritize a long list of options
Voting	• fast • high quality with dialogue • clear outcome	• may be too fast • winners and losers • no dialogue • influenced choices	• trivial matter • when there are clear options • if division of group is okay
Consensus Building	• collaborative • systematic • participative • discussion-oriented • encourages commitment	• takes time • requires data and member skills	• important issues • when total buy-in matters

....

Understanding Consensus Building

The crucial importance of consensus simply cannot be overstated and must be fully understood by all facilitators. At its core,

Facilitating is a consensual activity.

Besides being the #1 choice as a decision mode for all important decisions, facilitators are constantly building consensus with everything they do.

The following are all examples of consensus activities:

- summarizing a complex set of ideas to the satisfaction of group members
- getting everyone's input into a clear goal and objectives for the group's activities
- gaining buy-in from all members to the purpose of the session
- linking people's ideas together so they feel they're saying the same thing
- making notes on a flip chart in such a way that at the end of the discussion each member sees where and how they've contributed and is satisfied with what has been recorded
- discussing and agreeing on which decision mode to use in a formal decision-making process.

Since all facilitation activities must strive to be collaborative, participative, synergistic and unifying, all facilitation activities are essentially consensus building in nature!

....

Hallmarks of the Consensus Process

Regardless of whether consensus is being used formally to reach a decision on a specific issue, or informally as an ongoing facilitation technique, you know the group is working consensually if the following conditions are met:

- there are lots of ideas being shared
- discussion is based more on facts than feelings
- everyone is heard
- there's active listening and paraphrasing to clarify ideas and ideas are built on by other members
- no one is trying to push a pre-determined solution; instead there's an open and objective quest for solutions
- when the final solution is reached people feel satisfied that they were part of the decision
- everyone feels so consulted and involved that even though the final solution isn't the one they would have chosen working on their own, they can readily "live with it."

There are many situations where the decisions being made are of such magnitude that consensus needs to be designated as the only acceptable method of decision-making. In these cases, the group agrees to keep discussing until everyone indicates that they can live with the outcome.

Insisting on consensus is a wise strategy in situations where one or more individuals routinely dissent. If voting is used in these cases, the dissenters lose the vote and are then able to say that they weren't in agreement. This divides the group, allows dissenters to remain entrenched in their opinions and absolves them of responsibility for the outcomes decided by the group.

Working toward consensus forces dissenters to collaborate. If they refuse and consensus isn't reached because of specific individuals, the minutes should reflect who blocked progress.

You should not end a consensus exercise by asking, "Is everyone happy?" or even, "Does everyone agree?" At the end of even a great consensus process, people have usually made concessions, and are likely not getting everything they 'wanted'.

Consensus isn't designed to make people happy or leave them in 100% agreement. Its goal is to create an outcome that represents the best feasible course of action given the circumstances.

Don't ask
"Do we all agree?" or *"Is everyone happy?"*

Instead ask
"Have we got a well-thought-out solution that we all can live with and commit to implementing?"

Things to Watch for in Decision Making

Decision making is rarely easy. Following are some extra tips to help you manage decision-making sessions.

___ Be clear on the process to be used right upfront.

Explain any tools or techniques that will be used

___ Ask people what assumptions they're operating under either about the issue, or the organizational constraints. Note these and test them with the rest of the group.

___ Conflict is a natural part of the many decision-making discussions. Always confront differences assertively and collaboratively. Don't strive to avoid conflict or accommodate by asking people to be nice and get along.

___ Urge people not to give in if they feel they have important ideas. When everyone agrees so as not to offend anyone, "group think" is the result and poor decisions are made.

___ If the group has chosen to go for consensus because the issue is important, stick with it even if the going gets tough. Beware of the tendency to start voting, coin tossing and bargaining to make things easier.

___ Be very particular about achieving closure on each decision. Test for consensus and make sure things are final before moving on to other topics.

___ Stop the action if the process or behaviors become ineffective. Ask: *"What are we doing well? What aren't we doing so well?"* and *"What do we need to do about it?"* Then act on the suggestions for improvement.

Effective Decision Making Behaviors

To make any decision process work, group members need to behave themselves in certain specific ways. These behaviors can be shared with the group or generated as norms in advance of any decision making session.

Behaviors that Help	Behaviors that Hinder
Listening to other's ideas politely, even when you don't agree	Interrupting people in mid-sentence
Paraphrasing the main points made by another person, especially if you're about to contradict their ideas	Not acknowledging the ideas that others have put on the table
Praising other's ideas	Criticizing other's ideas, as opposed to giving them useful feedback
Building on other's ideas	Pushing your own ideas while ignoring other's input
Asking others to critique your ideas, and accepting the feedback	Getting defensive when your ideas are analyzed
Being open to accepting alternative courses of action	Sticking only to your ideas and blocking suggestions for alternatives
Dealing with facts	Basing arguments on feelings
Staying calm and friendly towards colleagues	Getting overly emotional; showing hostility in the face of any disagreement

Chapter 7
Meeting Management

"Oh no, not another meeting!!!"

*I*f you hear this every time a
meeting is called, there may be
some real meeting design issues
that you need to address. As facilitator, it's your job to help others
learn how to work effectively in order to
achieve their goals.

Use the following checklist to pinpoint some of the
common elements of ineffective meetings:

— meeting goal is unclear for some members
— a vague or nonexistent agenda
— no time limits on discussions
— no process for working on important issues
— no one facilitating discussions
— people haven't done their homework
— discussions go in circles
— lack of closure to discussions
— people argue rather than debate points of view
— a few people dominating while others sit passively
— meetings that end without detailed action plans
  for next steps
— absence of any process checking of the meeting
  as it unfolds, or any evaluation at the end

Meetings That Work

By contrast, here are the ingredients shared by all effective meetings:

✎ — a detailed agenda that spells out what will be discussed, the goal of the discussion, who is bringing that item forward and an estimate of how long each item will take

— clear process notes that describe the tools and techniques that will be used

— assigned roles such as facilitator, chairperson, minute taker, and timekeeper

— a set of group norms created by the members and posted in the meeting room

— clarity about decision making options and how they will be used

— effective member behaviors

— periodic process checks to make sure progress is being made

— clear conflict management strategies

— a process that creates true closure

— detailed and clear minutes

— specific follow-up plans

— a post-meeting evaluation

Special Note: _Previously, we've discussed such factors as setting group norms, decision-making options, effective member behaviors and conflict management. In this chapter you'll learn about other factors (such as agenda design) that are essential to making meetings work._

There are a number of symptoms of ineffective meetings. Once you learn them, think of them as a set of early warning signals against which to periodically check how healthy your own meetings are.

You can use this questionnaire to assess the overall quality of past meetings. Then use the survey feedback method described in Chapter 8.

✎ Meeting Diagnostic Survey

1. People tend to resist the idea of another meeting.

1	2	3	4	5
Totally	Disagree	Doesn't apply/ not sure	Agree	Totally agree

2. Meetings generally do not start or end on time.

1	2	3	4	5
Totally	Disagree	Doesn't apply/ not sure	Agree	Totally agree

3. When a member offers an idea, other members do not ask detailed questions or demonstrate active listening.

1	2	3	4	5
Totally	Disagree	Doesn't apply/ not sure	Agree	Totally agree

4. Discussions begin before it's clear to everyone exactly what is being discussed.

1	2	3	4	5
Totally	Disagree	Doesn't apply/ not sure	Agree	Totally agree

5. One or two members dominate the meeting.

1	2	3	4	5
Totally	Disagree	Doesn't apply/ not sure	Agree	Totally agree

6. Often the meeting ends before everyone has been heard from.

1	2	3	4	5
Totally	Disagree	Doesn't apply/ not sure	Agree	Totally agree

7. People do not address each other directly, but talk about others as if they were not in the room.

1	2	3	4	5
Totally	Disagree	Doesn't apply/ not sure	Agree	Totally agree

8. If the objective of the meeting hasn't been reached, a follow-up meeting is scheduled rather than run overtime.

1	2	3	4	5
Totally	Disagree	Doesn't apply/ not sure	Agree	Totally agree

9. Many ideas have to be repeated several times before they get a response.

1	2	3	4	5
Totally	Disagree	Doesn't apply/ not sure	Agree	Totally agree

10. The formal leader or chair seems to have more weight than other members.

1	2	3	4	5
Totally	Disagree	Doesn't apply/ not sure	Agree	Totally agree

11. People start to disagree before they really understand the full scope of what the other person is trying to say.

1	2	3	4	5
Totally	Disagree	Doesn't apply/ not sure	Agree	Totally agree

12. Following meetings, there are postmortems behind closed doors about what really went on.

1	2	3	4	5
Totally	Disagree	Doesn't apply/ not sure	Agree	Totally agree

13. There's never any assessment at the end of meetings to see if the group has achieved what it set out to do.

1	2	3	4	5
Totally	Disagree	Doesn't apply/ not sure	Agree	Totally agree

14. People react to new ideas by making fun, uttering put downs, or ignoring the idea all together rather than questioning and exploring it further.

1	2	3	4	5
Totally	Disagree	Doesn't apply/ not sure	Agree	Totally agree

15. Too many people sit in the meetings not really participating.

1	2	3	4	5
Totally	Disagree	Doesn't apply/ not sure	Agree	Totally agree

16. After the meeting, there's always some confusion about what was agreed upon and who is responsible for implementation.

1	2	3	4	5
Totally	Disagree	Doesn't apply/ not sure	Agree	Totally agree

17. Few decisions are made by consensus; the group lets individuals make decisions, or it tends to vote on issues without any preceding discussion/analysis.

1	2	3	4	5
Totally	Disagree	Doesn't apply/ not sure	Agree	Totally agree

18. The group cannot make decisions because it doesn't have the necessary information, or people haven't done their homework.

1	2	3	4	5
Totally	Disagree	Doesn't apply/ not sure	Agree	Totally agree

19. There's seldom any checking to see if the group has gone off track, or if the meeting is an effective use of time.

1	2	3	4	5
Totally	Disagree	Doesn't apply/ not sure	Agree	Totally agree

20. Too often we agree on a course of action because everyone is tired, or can not be bothered to delve deeper.

1	2	3	4	5
Totally	Disagree	Doesn't apply/ not sure	Agree	Totally agree

21. People seem to leave the meeting drained of energy.

1	2	3	4	5
Totally	Disagree	Doesn't apply/ not sure	Agree	Totally agree

22. The members seem to spend a disproportionate amount of time at the start of meetings trying to define the problem they're supposed to be working on.

1	2	3	4	5
Totally	Disagree	Doesn't apply/ not sure	Agree	Totally agree

23. During meetings people arrive late, ask to be excused early, are frequently called out and so on.

1	2	3	4	5
Totally	Disagree	Doesn't apply/ not sure	Agree	Totally agree

24. Arguments that have no real bearing on the topic of the meeting often break out.

1	2	3	4	5
Totally	Disagree	Doesn't apply/ not sure	Agree	Totally agree

25. When a serious conflict occurs between some members, no one in the group attempts to help.

1	2	3	4	5
Totally	Disagree	Doesn't apply/ not sure	Agree	Totally agree

Our Meetings Are Terrible!

Below are some of the symptoms of dysfunctional meetings and prescriptions for their cure. These are of course easier to identify than to fix, but if you can help team members become aware of their patterns, they can begin to resolve them.

SYMPTOMS	CURES
As each person finishes speaking, the next person starts a new topic. There is no building on ideas, thus no continuity of discussion. This results in a half-dozen topics in the air.	Have each person acknowledge the comments of the last speaker. Make it a rule to finish a point before moving forward.
People argue their side, trying to convince others that they're right rather than understanding either the issue or anyone else's input. There is no listening.	Train members to paraphrase what's said in response to their point. Record all sides of the issue on a flip chart. Once everyone understands these differing views, try for a decision.
As soon as a problem is mentioned, someone announces that they understand the problem. A solution is very quickly proposed and the discussion moves to another topic.	Use cause and effect diagrams or systematic problem solving to bring structure to meetings. Become thorough in solving problems. Avoid jumping to obvious solutions.
Whenever someone disagrees with a group decision, the dissenting view is ignored.	Develop an ear for dissenting views and make sure they get heard. Have someone else paraphrase the dissenting opinion.
The group uses brainstorming and voting to reach all decisions.	Preplan meeting processes so other tools are on hand, and then use them.

SYMPTOMS	CURES
Conversations often go nowhere for twenty to thirty minutes. In frustration the group goes on to another topic.	Set a time limit on each discussion and halfway through evaluate how it's going. Use periodic summaries, push for closure
People often become emotional. Sometimes they even say things to others that are quite personal.	Have people stop and rephrase their comments so there are no distracting personal innuendoes
Group members hold frequent side meetings to discuss what they're thinking. No one says any of this out loud of course.	Encourage honesty by valuing all input. Draw side chatterers back to the general conversation.
Group members don't notice they've become sidetracked on an issue until they've been off topic for quite awhile.	Call "sidetrack" or have some other signal to flag it. Decide if you want to digress or park the particular issue.
Only the real extroverts, or those with "power," do most of the talking. Some team members say little at most meetings.	Use round robins to get input. Call on members by name. Use idea slips to get written comments from everyone.
No one pays attention to body language. Some people have tuned out or even seem agitated.	Make perception checks and ask people to express their feelings.
There is no closure to most topics. Little action takes place between meetings.	Stress closure. Reach a clear decision and record it. Have an action planning form handy. Bring actions forward at the next meeting.
There is little achieved week after week.	Do a meeting evaluation. Discuss results before the next meeting. Post any new rules or improvement ideas.

The Fundamentals of Meeting Management

Create and Use a Detailed Agenda

Each meeting must have an agenda that's been developed ahead of time and ratified by the members of the team. By having the agenda in advance of the meeting, members can do their homework and come prepared to make decisions.

Agendas should include the following items:

__ topics for discussion, plus a brief description of what is involved and what needs to be accomplished

__ a time guideline for each item

__ the name of the person bringing forward the item

__ the details of the process to be used for each discussion

If the agenda cannot be designed in advance for whatever reason, then the first order of business at the meeting must be agenda building. In this facilitated discussion, members design the agenda for that day's session.

Develop Step-By-Step Process Notes

Most of the books that have been written on meetings do not mention 'process notes,' largely because these books are geared toward meetings that will be chaired rather than facilitated.

When a meeting is facilitated, there must be detailed process notes for each agenda item. These notes specify how the discussion will be facilitated. They specify the tools and techniques to be used, and how participation will be managed.

In the following sample agenda we've added process notes to illustrate their important role. While some facilitators keep these design notes to themselves, it's often a good idea to enhance buy-in to a process by openly sharing the process with the group.

Sample agenda with process notes

Name of group:	Customer Fulfillment Team
Members:	Jane, Muhammed, Jacques, Elaine, Carl, Fred, Diane, Joe
Meeting details:	Monday, June 12, 1999, 11:00 to 1:00 (Brown Bag Lunch), Conference Room C

What & Why*	How (process notes)
Warm up (10 min.) – Joe → To create focus	• Members share one recent customer contact story
Review agenda and norms (5 min) — Joe → To set context	• Ratify the agenda and the norms through general discussion. Add any new items. Make sure there is clarity about the overall goal of the meeting
Bring forward action items (25 min) — All → To implement monitoring	• Brief report by all members on action plans created at th last meeting. Add any new plans

What & Why*	How (process notes)
Focus group updates (20 min) — Jacques & Diane → To identify areas for improvement	• Report on outcomes of six customer focus groups. Use Forcefield Analysis to distinguish between what you're doing well and what you aren't
Prioritization of customer issues (20 min) — Joe → To set priorities	• Establish criteria to evaluate customer concerns • Use criteria matrix to appraise each issue and determine top priorities for action
Problem solving of priority issues (30 min) — Entire group → To create improvement plans	• Divide into two subteams to problem solve the two top priority issues; create detailed action plans for the top issues; meet as a group to share and ratify ideas
Next-step planning & agenda building (10 min) — Joe → To ensure closure and design next session	• Make sure everyone knows what they're expected to work on; start to form agenda for the next meeting
Exit survey (10 min) — Joe → To check meeting effectiveness	• Have everyone evaluate the meeting on their way out the door. List items to be brought forward at the next meeting

*Note: *Times given above are totally speculative and are only included for illustration purposes.*

Clarify Roles and Responsibilities

Effective meetings require people to play defined roles

Facilitator: designs the methodology for the meeting, manages participation, offers useful tools, helps the group determine its needs, keeps things on track and periodically checks on how things are going. A facilitator doesn't offer opinions about what is being discussed, but instead focuses on how issues are being discussed. A facilitator is a procedural expert who is there to help and support the group's effectiveness. Facilitation is focused on asking.

Chairperson: runs the meeting according to defined rules, but also offers opinions and engages in the discussion if he or she chooses. The chairperson has traditionally not been neutral. Most often, the chairperson of any meeting is the official leader, who plays an active role as decision maker and 'opinion leader.'

Minute taker: takes brief, accurate notes of what is discussed and the decisions made. Also responsible for incorporating the notes on flip charts. Most often, minute-taking responsibilities are rotated among the regular members of a work group. However, for special meetings or if money is not a barrier, this role can be played by someone not involved in the discussion.

Timekeeper: a rotating role in which someone keeps track of the time and reminds the group periodically if they're staying within guidelines. Not a license to be autocratic or shut down important discussions if they're running over. The use of an automatic timer will let the timekeeper participate in the discussion more comfortably.

Scribe: a group member who volunteers to write/record comments on a flip chart. Some facilitators are more comfortable asking others to make notes on the flip chart while they facilitate. This has the benefit of freeing the facilitator from the distractions of writing, but adds its own complications. The scribe may start facilitating or may not make the notes the way the facilitator wants. Having a scribe takes a lot of coordination. Since a scribe takes a second person out of the discussion, a general rule is that a facilitator should make his or her own notes if at all possible. If a scribe is used, clarifying questions should be channeled through the facilitator, instead of the scribe interacting directly with the members.

Balancing the roles of chairperson and facilitator

Chairing and facilitating are two distinct meeting management styles. Each has its strengths and its place.

Chairing is most useful at the start of a meeting in order to go over minutes, share information and manage a round robin report-back by members. Chairing traditionally relies on the use of "Parliamentary Rules of Order".

Since chairs are not neutral, their major drawback is that they tend to influence decisions and concentrate power. It's not uncommon for a strong chairperson to make final decisions on important items.

A consequence of this decision mode is that the chair

'owns' the outcome. There is also little emphasis on using process tools when playing the traditional role of the chairperson.

Facilitating is designed to foster the full and equal participation of all members when their input is needed to decide issues. Since facilitators are neutral, they empower members. They rely on consensus and collaboration to reach important decisions. This results in decisions for which the whole group feels it has ownership.

Facilitation creates rules from within the group, rather than imposing rules from a book. Facilitation is also associated with a rich array of tools and techniques designed to create synergy and get better ideas.

A very common role arrangement is to have a meeting leader who uses a chairperson approach to start the meeting, deal with the agenda, take care of the housekeeping and information sharing portions of the session and then switch to facilitation in order to get input on the discussion topics within the agenda.

All good facilitators should know when and how to act as an effective chairperson. Conversely, it would be ideal if all chairpersons were also skilled facilitators who could switch styles when they wanted to get participation and ownership.

With some planning beforehand, these roles won't conflict. The key is to remember that each has its place, and to be clear about which approach is being used.

In summary:

Chair when you want to	Facilitate when you want to
• review past minutes and agenda items	• increase participation
• exchange information	• shift ownership
• hear members report back	• get members to make decisions
• discuss next steps	• get members to create action plans

4. Set Clear Meeting Norms

Make sure that the group has clear norms for behavior and that those norms are created by the group. Help the group tailor their norms to meet the demands of particular meetings by helping them set targeted norms if applicable (refer to Targeted Norms, pg. 45).

5. Manage Participation

Make sure that everyone is part of the discussion, structure exists for each item and there is an effective use of decision-making tools to bring closure to all items.

As facilitator, you are responsible for ensuring that members know and exhibit effective discussion skills. If members are not skilled, then you should conduct the training exercises suggested on pg. 53, or use other strategies discussed in that chapter.

6. Make Periodic Process Checks

Process checking is a technique that every facilitator should utilize during meetings to keep meetings from going 'off the rails'. It involves stopping the discussion and turning the group's attention to how the meeting is going. The purpose of this shift in focus is to engage members in checking how things are being done and what changes are needed to improve the flow of the meeting.

There are Four Basic Elements in Process Checking:

1. Check for progress: Ask members if they think the goals are being achieved. Are problems being solved? Are decisions being made?

When to check progress: If things seem to be getting stuck; at points of closure; at least once per session.

2. Check the pace: Ask if things are moving too quickly or too slowly. Get any suggestions for improving the pace, and implement these immediately.

When to check the pace: When things seem to be dragging or moving too fast; any time people look frustrated; at least once per session/meeting.

3. Check the process: Ask members if the tool or approach being used is working or needs to be changed. Ask for or offer suggestions for another approach.

When to check the process: When the tool isn't yielding the results you hoped for, or it's evident that the process isn't being followed as laid out.

4. Take the pulse: Ask members how they're feeling. Are they energized? Tired? Do they feel satisfied, frustrated? Ask for their suggestions on how to perk things up.

When to take the pulse: Any time members look

distracted, tired or frustrated; at least once during each session.

How to do a Process Check

Process checks can be done verbally by asking members directly or in written form by posting the survey below on a flip chart. Members can then anonymously rate how the meeting is going thus far. When members return from the break, ask them to interpret the survey results and brainstorm ideas for improving the remainder of the session. Act on their suggestions immediately.

Sample Process Check Survey

Tell us how it's going so far with …

Progress: To what extent are we achieving our goals?

1	2	3	4	5
Poor	Fair	Satisfactory	Good	Excellent

Pace: How does the pace feel?

1	2	3	4	5
Far too slow	Slow	Just right	Fast	Far too fast

Process: Are we using the right methods/tools?

1	2	3	4	5
Not at all		Somewhat		Extremely effective

Pulse: How are you feeling about the session? Put a check mark beside any that describe you now.

1	2	3	4	5
Totally frustrated	Exhausted	Satisfied	Pleased	Energized

7. Take Minutes

Assign someone in the group to take very brief, concise notes. The best minutes are short one-page summaries of what was decided and next steps.

8. Determine Next Steps

Never let a group leave a meeting without clear next steps in place. Define what will be done, by whom and when. These action plans need to be brought forward at all subsequent meetings to ensure that the group is following through on commitments.

9. Evaluate the Meeting

Always get the group to review and evaluate each meeting. This evaluation should include what can be done to improve the next meeting and some feedback for the facilitator.

There are three ways to evaluate a meeting:

Forcefield Analysis – Ask the following:

"What were the strengths of today's meeting?" **(+)**
"What were the weaknesses?" **(-)**
*"What should we do to correct the
weaknesses?"* **(Rx)**

Exit Survey – Three to six questions are written on a sheet of flip-chart paper, and posted near an exit. Members fill it out upon leaving the meeting. Results are discussed at the start of the next meeting. On the next page you'll find a sample Meeting Exit Survey.

Formal Survey – Hand the survey out to members to

complete. After being tabulated, the results are discussed at a subsequent meeting. This is an appropriate exercise to be done three or four times a year for any ongoing group or team. A sample Meeting Effectiveness Survey is provided on the next page. The Survey Feedback process is described in Chapter 8 of this book.

Sample Meeting Exit Survey

Give us your assessment of the items below.

Output: How well did we achieve what we needed to?

1	2	3	4	5
Poor	Fair	Satisfactory	Good	Excellent

Use of time: How well did we use our time?

1	2	3	4	5
Poor	Fair	Satisfactory	Good	Excellent

Participation: How well did we ensure everyone was equally involved?

1	2	3	4	5
Poor	Fair	Satisfactory	Good	Excellent

Decision-making: How well-thought-out were our decisions?

1	2	3	4	5
Poor	Fair	Satisfactory	Good	Excellent

Action Plans: How clear and doable are our action plans?

1	2	3	4	5
Poor	Fair	Satisfactory	Good	Excellent

Organization: How well run was the meeting?

1	2	3	4	5
Poor	Fair	Satisfactory	Good	Excellent

✎ Meeting Effectiveness Survey

Instructions: Please give your candid opinions of the meetings you attended as part of this group. Rate the characteristic of the meetings by circling the appropriate number on each scale to represent your evaluation. Remain anonymous.
Return the survey to your group facilitator. Remember, you ar rating the meetings of this group.

1. Meeting Objectives
Are objectives clearly set out in advance of the meeting

1	2	3	4	5	6	7

Objectives are seldom
set out in advance

Objectives are alwa
set out in advanc

2. Communication
Are agendas circulated to all members in advance of the meeting?

1	2	3	4	5	6	7

Agendas are rarely
circulated in advance

Agendas are alwa
circulated in advanc

3. Start Times
Do meetings start on time?

1	2	3	4	5	6	7

Meeting hardly ever
start on time

Meetings always sta
on tim

4. Time Limits
Are time limits set for each agenda item?

1	2	3	4	5	6	7

We do not set
time limits

Time limits are alway
set for each ite

5. Meeting Review

Are action items from the previous meeting(s) brought forward?

1	2	3	4	5	6	7

Items are seldom brought forward

Items are always brought forward from previous meetings

6. Warm-up

Is there a meeting warm-up to hear from all members?

1	2	3	4	5	6	7

We seldom use a meeting warm-up

We often use a meeting warm-up

7. Role Clarity

Are roles (e.g. timekeeper, scribe, facilitator) made clear?

1	2	3	4	5	6	7

Roles are not identified

Roles are always clearly defined

8. Setting

Is there a quiet place for the meeting, with ample work space, flip charts and AV support?

1	2	3	4	5	6	7

The meeting place is not well suited

The meeting place is very good

9. Process

Is there clarity before each topic as to how that item will be managed?

1	2	3	4	5	6	7

There is rarely any planning on process

There is always clarity on process

10. Preparation
Does everyone come prepared and ready to make decisions?

1	2	3	4	5	6	7

We are often
unprepared

We are generall
prepare

11. Interruptions
Are meetings being disrupted due to people leaving, phones ringing, pagers beeping, etc.

1	2	3	4	5	6	7

There are constant
interruptions

We contr
interruption

12. Participation
Are all members fully exchanging views, taking responsibility for action items and follow-up?

1	2	3	4	5	6	7

People hold back and
don't take ownership

Everyone offers idea
and takes actio

13. Leadership
Does one person make all the decisions, or is there a sharing of authority?

1	2	3	4	5	6	7

The manager holds the chair
and makes most decisions

Authority is share

14. Pace
How would you rate the pace of the meetings?

1	2	3	4	5	6	7

Poor

Just rig

5. Tracking

Do meetings stay on track and follow the agenda?

1	2	3	4	5	6	7

Meeting usually stray off track   Meetings usually stay on track

6. Record Keeping

Are quality minutes kept and circulated?

1	2	3	4	5	6	7

Yes, they are   No, they are not

7. Listening

Do members practise active listening?

1	2	3	4	5	6	7

We don't listen closely to each other   Members listen actively

8. Conflict Management

Are differences of opinion suppressed, or is conflict effectively used?

1	2	3	4	5	6	7

Conflict isn't very effectively used   Conflict is effectively exploited for new ideas

9. Decision-Making

Does the group generally make good decisions at our meetings?

1	2	3	4	5	6	7

We tend to make poor decisions   We tend to make good decisions

20. Closure

Do we tend to end topics before getting into new ones

	I	2	3	4	5	6	7

We constantly start
new topics

We close each topi
before moving o

21. Consensus

Do we work hard to make collaborative decisions that
we can all live with?

	I	2	3	4	5	6	7

We abandon consensus
too easily

We work har
to reach consensu

22. Follow-up

Is there good coherent follow-up to commitments
made at meetings?

	I	2	3	4	5	6	7

We tend not to
follow-up

There is consisten
follow-u

Chapter 8
Process Tools for Facilitators

*I*magine a carpenter trying to build a house without the proper tools. It would certainly be ineffective if not all together impossible! Regardless of the job, you need the right tools. Fortunately for facilitators, there is a rich set of tools available.

Since dozens of tools exist, it would be impossible to explain them all. Only the most often used tools will be highlighted in this chapter. This set represents the basic processes that every facilitator must know how and when to use.

You'll find a detailed description of each on the following pages.

- Visioning
- Gap Analysis
- Decision Grids
- Priority Setting
- Systematic Problem Solving
- Survey Feedback
- Sequential Questioning
- Forcefield Analysis
- Multi-Voting
- Troubleshooting
- Needs and Offers Negotiation
- Brainstorming
- Root-Cause Analysis

In addition to these tools, all facilitators should learn the techniques associated with quality improvement such as process mapping, mind mapping, affinity diagrams, pare to analysis, tree diagrams, sequence flow charting, contro charts, storyboarding, SWAT analysis, histograms, scatter diagrams, flowcharts and critical path charts.

Visioning

What is it? A highly participative approach to goal setting for groups of anywhere from six to more than 100 members.

When should you use it? When members need to clarify their own thoughts and then share those idea with each other to create a clear shared statement of the desired future.

What is its purpose? Allows people to put forward their ideas. Makes sure everyone is involved and heard from. Creates energy. Gets people aligned. Gives people a creative method to identify a group goal

What's the outcome? This visioning process is very participative and energizes everyone in the room. It also creates buy-in because the group's direction is coming from the members themselves. Everyone is involved at once. All ideas are heard. It is a great way t conduct goal setting with a group.

How does Visioning work?

Step 1: Post a series of questions that relate to the task and ask how the final outcome ought to look at a future point in time. The vision questions will always be different, of course, depending on the situation.

> ### Sample Visioning Questions for a Customer Service Improvement Team
>
> Imagine that it's exactly two years from today:
>
> • *Describe how you now serve customers.*
>
> • *What specific improvements have been made?*
>
> • *What are people saying about the team now?*
>
> • *What problems has the group solved?*
>
> • *What specific outcomes have been achieved?*
>
> • *How are people behaving differently?*

Step 2: Ask each person to write down his/her own responses to the questions. Allow at least five minutes. Give more time if needed. Ask people not to speak to each other during this writing phase.

Step 3: Ask everyone to get a partner. Allocate three to five minutes for the first partner to share their vision. Ask the other partner to facilitate. After three to five minutes, ask the partners to switch roles so that the second person gets to talk.

Step 4: When time is up ask everyone to find another partner. Repeat the process outlined in Step 3, only allow slightly less time per person. Encourage people to 'steal' any good ideas they got from their last partner and incorporate these into their own vision.

Step 5: Repeat the process again with new partners. This time, limit the exchange to one to three minutes per person in order to force people to prioritize and share the highlights.

> ✓ Tip: You can keep switching partners until every one has spoken to everyone else. This creates lots of energy!

Step #6: Ask everyone to return to their original seats, and then begin facilitating a discussion to pull the ideas together. You'll find that ideas have become fairly homogenized by this point.

> ✓ Tip: A good way to proceed is question by question, having everyone read all their ideas on just that item. Then, ask people what themes they heard repeated and record them.

Sequential Questioning

What is it? An assessment exercise conducted in the form of a series of questions. These are posed to the whole group at the start of a workshop.

When should you use it? To uncover important information about the group, their issues or activities. To test and probe in a challenging manner. To raise issues and create discontent with the status quo.

What is its purpose? Yields information, lets you test assumptions and challenge people. Gets people to surface their negativity and cynicism. Vents negative feelings and creates an obvious need to take action. Helps the facilitator anticipate the issues that might come up throughout the day. When done well, this technique creates a shared desire to make change happen. It certainly warms up the group.

What is the outcome? Sequential questioning is a challenging technique that creates sparks. It raises issues and gets people talking about the barriers. It raises people's consciousness about what the important problems are. It sets the stage for problem solving and solution development.

Since there is potential for disagreement, if you plan to use sequential questioning, you have to be prepared to make interventions and manage any conflicts that arise.

How does Sequential Questioning work?

Step 1: Analyze the overall topic and create about ten questions working from macro to micro issues. Each question should probe the situation in a challenging way so that the ensuing discussion reveals honest information important to the issue at hand.

Step 2: Write only one question at the top of each sheet of flip chart paper. Use the rest of the sheet to record reactions. Do not let people see the questions until you pose them. As you turn over each sheet, ask only one person in the group to respond. Record their response. Then, invite others to add their thoughts.

> ✓ Tip: Build questions around issues people identified in preworkshop interviews. Pose them as close-ended questions or items to be rated on a scale. Choose someone to answer

yes or no, to each item. Then ask others if they agree. Discuss people's reasons for their answer until you and the group can formulate a summary statement about how everyone feels about each question.

While sample questions are offered on the next page remember that these questions always need to be created to fit each particular situation.

Sample Sequential Questions

Workshop: Focus on Business Improvement

Answer **yes** or **no**, then explain your response.

yes or **no**	The overall business environment for the next five years will be advantageous for our business.
Rationale➤	
yes or **no**	We are fully prepared to handle all the opportunities that will occur in the next five years.
Rationale➤	
yes or **no**	Our current business development strategy is dynamic and flexible enough to respond to constant changes in the business environment.
Rationale➤	
yes or **no**	Our business strategy should be developed by people at the higher levels.
Rationale➤	

yes or **no**   Our staff are ready and motivated to over come barriers.

Rationale▶

yes or **no**   We understand our customers' needs and wants.

Rationale▶

yes or **no**   We have an early warning and performance measurement system that lets us track our progress and make timely corrections.

Rationale▶

yes or **no**   There is a high level of harmony and cooperation that ensures synergy and team work inside our organization.

Rationale▶

yes or **no**   We have the best products on the market. We own the market in our field.

Rationale▶

yes or **no**   We have a fairly flawless delivery system for getting our product to our customers.

Rationale▶

yes or **no**   We often have creative business development discussions during our regular meetings. Better customer service is a topic we discuss all the time.

Rationale▶

Brainstorming

What is it? A technique for getting bigger and better ideas. Puts a full range of ideas on the table before decisions are made.

When should you use it? To generate a free flow of creative ideas that are not bound by the usual barriers. To get everyone involved. To create energy. To generate a wide range of solutions for a problem.

What is its purpose? Allows people to explore new ideas and challenge traditional thinking. Lets people put ideas on the table without fear of being corrected or challenged. It separates the creation of ideas from the evaluation activity.

What is the outcome? A long list of creative ideas from which to work. Since brainstorming frees people from practical considerations it encourages them to think creatively. It's also an energizing process that helps move people to take action. Because it's highly participative, brainstorming makes everyone feel that they're an important part of the solution.

How does Brainstorming work?

Step 1: Announce that you will be using brainstorming. Review the rules:

- Let ideas flow freely
- No evaluating of ideas until later
- Build on the ideas of others
- Be humorous and creative

- There are no bad ideas
- No debating
- Everyone participates

- Think in new ways; break out of old patterns
- Keep discussion moving

Step 2: Clarify the topic being brainstormed, then allow a few minutes of silence while people think about solutions.

Step 3: Ask members to let their ideas flow. The actual brainstorming can be structured (go systematically around the group) or be spontaneous (members offer ideas as they come to mind).

Step 4: Record ideas as they're generated. Do not discuss or elaborate on them. Keep it moving.

Step 5: When people have run out of ideas, allow for a few minutes of thinking time and reflection. Sometimes the best ideas emerge in the second round.

Step 6: When there really are no further suggestions, discuss each brainstormed idea in detail so that it's fully developed and clearly understood. Combine similar ideas that are simply worded differently.

Step 7: Use a decision grid (pg. 147) or multi-voting (pg. 141) to sort the good ideas from the poor ones.

Step 8: Agree on the final list of best ideas.

Anonymous Brainstorming

What is it? An idea generation technique that asks people to write down their ideas, then pass them to other group members who build on them.

When should you use it? When people are reluctant to speak in front of others, or when there are outspoken members who would dominate a verbal brainstorming session. It's also useful if the issue or topic is sensitive, since the initial idea generation step is anonymous and private.

What is its purpose? The anonymity of this tool gives people the freedom to express their ideas.

What's the outcome? Idea building generates lots of ideas. It also allows people to build on each other's ideas in an anonymous setting.

How does Anonymous Brainstorming work?

Step 1: Clarify the topic or issue for which ideas will be generated. Explain the process to members.

Step 2: Give each person small slips of paper. Ask members to work alone as they think of ideas to resolve the issue being discussed. Allow anywhere from three to 10 minutes for the idea generation step.

Step 3: Ask members to fold their idea sheets and toss them into the center of the table. (Slips should not have names on them.)

Step 4: Mix the sheets and ask each person to take back as many as they tossed in. If anyone pulls out his/her own slip, that person can toss it back, or exchange it with a neighbor.

Step 5: Each person now has five to 10 minutes to add his or her thoughts to build on the original idea on

ach sheet picked from the pile. The slips can then be
assed to a third person to generate further ideas.

tep 6: Once all ideas have been developed, ask all
embers to read their suggestions out loud.

tep 7: Discuss ideas and record them on the flip
hart.

tep 8: Use a decision grid (pg. 147) or multi-voting
g. 141) to find the best ideas to fit the situation.

orcefield Analysis

What is it? Forcefield analysis is a structured
ethod of looking at the two opposing forces acting on
situation.

When should you use it? When you need to sur-
ace all of the factors at play in a situation, so that barri-
rs and problems can be identified.

What is its purpose? Clarifies the resources avail-
ble, and also the barriers or obstacles. Helps groups
nderstand what they need to do to succeed.

What is the outcome? Forcefield is a valuable
ool for analyzing situations and identifying problems
hat need to be solved. It helps groups make more effec-
ve decisions because it lets members look at both pos-
ive and negative forces at play.

ow does Forcefield Analysis work?

tep 1: Identify a topic, situation or project, such as
ay, computer training.

Step 2: Help the group state the goal. Example: "All staff will receive training in the new operating system in three weeks."

Step 3: Draw a line down the centre of a flip chart sheet. Use one side to identify all of the forces (resources, skills, attitudes) that will help reach the goal. On the other side, identify all the forces that could hinder reaching the goal (barriers, problems, deficiencies, etc.)

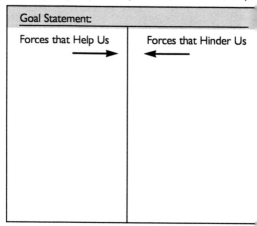

Goal Statement:	
Forces that Help Us	Forces that Hinder Us
→	←

Step 4: Once all help and hinder items have been identified, use a decision matrix or multi-voting (see this chapter) to determine which of the hindrances or barriers are a priority for immediate problem solving.

Step 5: Address the priority barriers using the

Variations of Forcefield Analysis

Forcefield has a number of variations. Each one has been created using roughly the same steps as described previously.

These variations include the following items:

✓ Pros	✗ Cons
✓ Things we are doing well	✗ Things we could do better
✓ Hopes	✗ Fears
✓ Best case scenario	✗ Worst case scenario
✓ Assets	✗ Liabilities
✓ Strengths	✗ Weaknesses
✓ Positives	✗ Negatives
✓ Opportunities	✗ Obstacles

Gap Analysis

What is it? A means of identifying blocks to achieving a desired goal.

When should you use it? When a group needs to understand the gap between where they currently are and where they ultimately want to end up.

What is its purpose? Gap analysis lets you explore the missing steps between where you are and where you want to go. It forces a realistic look at the present and helps identify the things that need to be done to arrive at the desired future.

What is the outcome? Gap analysis is a planning tool that creates alignment between group members as to what needs to be done to eliminate the gap between where they currently are (present state) and where they ideally would like to be (desired future state).

How does Gap Analysis work?

Step 1: Identify the future state. Use visioning or any other approach that yields a picture of where the group wants to be at a specific time. The description of the future must be detailed. Post the information on the right-hand side of a large work space on a wall.

Step 2: Identify the present state. How are things now? Describe the same components featured in the future state, only do so in real, present terms. Again be very detailed. Post the ideas generated on the left-hand side of the wall work space.

Step 3: Focus on the gaps. Ask members to work with a partner to discuss the following points:

- What are the gaps?
- What are the barriers?
- What's missing?

Step 4: Share ideas as a group and post these on the wall between the 'present' and the 'future.'

Step 5: Once there is consensus on the gaps, divide the large group into subgroups and give each group one or more gap items to problem solve.

Step 6: Reassemble the whole group to hear recommendations and action plans.

Step 7: Ratify the plans by getting acceptance from all other members, then create a mechanism for follow-up.

Present State	Gap	Desired Future
Teams operate without leaders for months because there aren't enough people trained	No team leader training program	A trained cadre of team leaders

Multi-Voting

What is it? A decision-making tool that enables a group to sort through a long list of ideas to identify priorities.

When should you use it? When a group has to discuss a long list of items and then has to quickly identify which one(s) should be dealt with immediately.

What is its purpose? Quickly establishes a clear set of priorities.

What is the outcome? Multi-voting is democratic and participative. Since most members will see at least one or more of the items that they voted for near the top of the priority list, this form of voting does not create the sense of winners and losers that majority voting does.

How does Multi-Voting work?

Step 1: Clarify the items being prioritized, which may include a list of barriers from a Forcefield analysis or a list of ideas from a Brainstorming exercise. Have members discuss each item, what it means, its strengths and weaknesses and so on to make sure people understand the choices they're making.

Step 2: Identify some criteria to guide the vote more specifically so that people don't vote at cross purposes. Make sure that everyone votes with the same criteria in mind. The criteria could be one or more of the following

- the lowest cost items
- the easiest items to complete
- the first items in a logical sequence
- the most important items
- the most innovative items
- the most important to the customer

Step 3: Once the criteria are clear, there are two methods for conducting a multi-vote.

Method 1: Voting with Sticker Dots

- Using colored, peel-off file-folder dots, hand out a strip of four to seven dots to each person. Use slightly less dots than half the items to be sorted to force people to make choices (e.g. give out four dots to sort 10 items).
- Ask members to put four stickers on their top four choices listed on the flip chart. (Ensure that no one puts all four stickers on one choice.)
- When everyone has voted, tally the dots in order to arrive at the priorities.

Method 2: Distributing Points

- Give each person points (usually 10 or 100) to distribute among the items to be sorted.
- Members then place their points beside the items they favor. It's wise not to allow anyone to place more than 50 percent of their points on any single item.
- When everyone has voted, tally the points in order to arrive at the priorities.

Root-Cause Analysis

What is it? A systematic analysis of an issue to identify the root causes rather than the symptoms.

When should you use it? When you need to delve beneath surface symptoms and uncover the underlying causes of problems.

What is its purpose? Leads to more complete and final solutions.

What is the outcome? Root-cause analysis forces groups to look more deeply at problems and to deal with the underlying causes. This often means that problems are more likely to be resolved once and for all.

How does Root-Cause Analysis work?

Step 1: Explain the difference between 'causes' and their 'effects' to group members. For example, you can ask whether a noisy muffler is a cause or an effect. Once people have identified that it's an effect, ask them to list all of the causes. Point out that effects can't be solved, but underlying causes can.

Step 2: You now have a choice of two basic methods, as described below, for determining root cause(s): Cause & Effect Charting or Fishbone Diagrams.

Step 3: Once all causes are identified, brainstorm solutions for each one.

Method 1: Cause and Effect Charting

- When analyzing a problem, divide a flip-chart sheet in two and write effects on the right side and causes on the left. Example: Noisy Muffler.

Cause	Effect
• corrosion	• noise and fumes
• loose clamps	when accelerating
• puncture	

- Whenever anyone offers a point of analysis ask them if it's a cause or effect. Write each item in its appropriate column. Probe each item in the effect column to determine what causes it. Continue until all causes have been identified.

Method 2: Fishbone Diagrams

Use a fishbone diagram to systematically sort all of the contributing causes for the problem being analyzed. The cause categories on fishbone charts vary, but usually include people, machinery/equipment, methods, materials, policies, environment and measurement. The number of categories will vary.

- Start by placing the observed effect in the 'head' of

the fishbone. Determine the major cause categories, then ask members to brainstorm all of the possible causes on each 'rib' of the fish. Example:

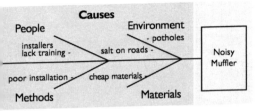

- Once all of the causes have been identified, ask the group to brainstorm solutions for each of them, or use multi-voting to sort which causes are their highest priority for being solved.

Decision Grid

What is it? A matrix of critical criteria used to assess a set of ideas in order to determine which one(s) are most likely to offer the best solution(s).

When should you use it? When you need to bring more objectivity and thoroughness to the decision-making process.

What is its purpose? Changes the decision-making process from one where members debate which solutions they feel are most suitable, to one where each potential solution is objectively judged against the same set of criteria.

....

What is the outcome? Clear, sorted ideas emerge from a mass of random brainstormed thoughts. Grids also make the sorting process more systematic. Since everyone gets to cast votes or express opinions, the use of grids is participative and democratic.

How does the Decision Grid work?

Once members have brainstormed a set of ideas to solve a problem, create a decision grid. Two types of decision grids are illustrated: criteria based and impact/effort based.

Criteria-Based Grids

Step 1: Ask members to identify the criteria against which all of the potential solutions will be judged. Examples:

- saves time
- saves money
- reduces stress
- is timely
- is doable
- is affordable
- is fast
- supports the strategic plan
- is something we can control
- represents the right sequence
- builds empowerment
- will get management support
- satisfies customer needs
- doesn't disrupt our operation

Step 2: The top three to five criteria are chosen from this list and placed along the top of a grid. The options being considered are placed down the left column.

Step 3: Each option is then evaluated as to the extent to which it meets each criteria that the group has selected. Note that some criteria may be more impor-

....

tant than others, and hence given more weight.
Rate each solution against the criteria as follows:

$$1 = \text{does not meet the criteria}$$
$$2 = \text{somewhat meets the criteria}$$
$$3 = \text{good at meeting the criteria}$$

Step 4: Add up the scores to determine which solutions will be implemented.

Decision Grid Example:

Decision grid for assessing solutions to the challenge of getting 50 people training in new software within 14 days.

	Criteria				
	Cost Effective (x 1)	Meets Customer Needs** (x 3)	Speed (x 1)	Lack of Disruption (x 1)	Totals per Solution
Shut down to give each person two days classroom training	1 2 1 1 ÷ 4 = 1.25	1 1 1 1 ÷ 4 = 1.00	3 3 3 3 ÷ 4 = 3.00	1 1 1 1 ÷ 4 = 1.00	8.25
Have 10 experts on site for two weeks to give one-on-one support	2 2 2 1 ÷ 4 = 1.75	2 3 2 2 ÷ 4 = 2.25	1 2 1 1 ÷ 4 = 1.25	3 3 3 3 ÷ 4 = 3.00	12.75
Have 10 people off for training each two-day period	2 2 3 3 ÷ 4 = 2.50	2 3 3 2 ÷ 4 = 2.50	2 2 2 2 ÷ 4 = 2.00	2 2 2 3 ÷ 4 = 2.25	14.25

*Four individuals have rated here. The average was calculated by dividing the sum total of the ratings by the number of individuals participating ($1 + 2 + 1 + 1 ÷ 4 = 1.25$).

**If any of the criteria is more important than the others, it can be given a multiplier factor (i.e.: x 3). In the above example 'meets customers needs' is three times more important than the other criteria.

Step 5: Create action plans for top ranked items.

Impact/Effort-Based Grids

Step 1: Post all ideas on a nearby wall and draw the impact/effort grid on a sheet of flip-chart paper.

		– Effort –	
		Difficult To Do	Easy To Do
– Impact –	Major Improvement	3.	1.
	Minor Improvement	4.	2.

Step 2: Discuss the brainstormed ideas one by one and place each in one of the four boxes. All items are eventually classified in the following categories:

1. Easy to do and yields a big improvement
2. Easy to do but yields a small improvement
3. Difficult to do but yields a big improvement
4. Difficult to do but yields small improvement

Category 1 items are implemented immediately
Category 2 items are also implemented immediately
Category 3 items are the subject of detailed action
　　　　　　　planning
Category 4 items are discarded

The major difficulty in using an impact/effort grid lies in clarifying exactly what is meant by 'easy to do', 'difficult to do', 'small improvement' and 'big improvement.'

because everyone will understand these terms differently. Being clear at the start will avoid a lot of heated
debate later.

___**Special Note:**___ *Impact/Effort grids are easier to use
than criteria grids since there is no need to create criteria
and the grid has already been designed.*

Troubleshooting

What is it? A process for identifying potential problems and creating plans to overcome them.

When should you use it? When it's important to
identify barriers to success and create action plans to
deal with them.

What is its purpose? Helps a group make sure its
action plans are realistic and well thought out.

What is the outcome? Groups gain more control
over their activities in spite of a constantly changing and
challenging workplace. They're also less likely to be 'sur-
prised' by circumstances.

How does Troubleshooting work?

Step 1: After a group has created action plans, ask
them to consider a series of questions. These questions
force a critical look at the circumstances that might
impede the activity. For example:

- What are the difficult, complex or sensitive aspects of
  our action plan?
- What shifts in the environment, like a change of
  priorities, should we keep our eye on?

- What organizational blocks or barriers could we run into?
- What technical or materials-related problems could stop or delay us?
- What human resource issues should we be aware of at this point?
- In which ways might members of this team not fulfill their commitments?

Step 2: Once potential barriers have been identified, ask members to identify strategies and action plans to overcome each one.

Step 3: Have the group write its troubleshooting plans in detail. Identify who will monitor follow-through. The following work sheet should help you lead the discussion

Troubleshooting Worksheet

Activity Being Planned:

What could go wrong, block us or change suddenly?	What actions do we need to take to overcome each block? (what, how, by whom, when)

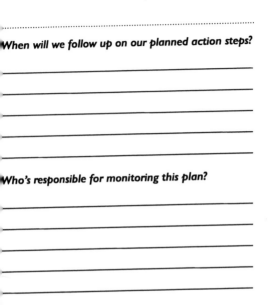

When will we follow up on our planned action steps?

_____

_____

_____

_____

_____

Who's responsible for monitoring this plan?

_____

_____

_____

_____

_____

Survey Feedback

What is it? A group process that involves gathering information and feeding it back to the members so that they can interpret the data and take actions they feel are appropriate.

When should you use it? When there is a problem that group members need to address but you lack specific information about the situation.

What is its purpose? It gives the group a means of assessing how it's doing and provides a method for creating actions to resolve any identified problems.

What is the outcome? Members (not the team leader or facilitator) interpret the survey results. This builds commitment and accountability. Members face the problems and deal with them in a productive manner.

How does it work?

Step 1: Design and conduct an anonymous survey. It can be about the following items:

- how meetings are run
- the effectiveness of the team
- the performance of the team leader
- the effectiveness of a process
- the satisfaction of customers

Step 2: After the surveys have been filled out, they are returned to a designated member of the group. This person tabulates the survey results by combining all of the responses onto one survey form. The person doing the tabulation doesn't interpret the results; he or she just accurately combines the ratings from the individual surveys.

Step 3: Share the tabulated survey results with the group at a meeting. After they have had an opportunity to read the results, ask them two questions:

> *"What is the survey data telling us is going well? Which items got high ratings?"*

> *"What is the survey data telling us is a problem or issue? Which items got low ratings?"**

*A rating is generally considered low if the ratings from 'satisfactory' downward are greater than the ratings for items four and five combined. In some cases (e.g. small groups) even one poor rating will indicate that the item needs attention.)

In the example below nine out of 14 ratings were scored equal to, or below satisfactory, which means that this item is a cause for concern.

poor		satisfactory		excellent
1	2	3	4	5
✗✗	✗✗✗	✗✗✗✗	✗✗✗	✗✗

Step 4: Once members have identified all of the items that received low enough ratings to be of concern, have them rank these in terms of priority to determine which should be dealt with right away.

Since not every issue can be problem solved, use multi-voting to determine this priority. Ask members this question:

"If we could only solve four of the problems identified, which four should we tackle first?"

Step 5: Once the top priorities are clear, divide the members into subgroups of no less than four individuals. Give each subgroup one issue to work on for about 20 minutes. Deal with as many issues as group size allows.

In subgroups, members will answer two sets of questions about the item they have been given:

"Why did this item get a low rating? What is wrong here? What is the nature of the problem?" (group members analyze the problem)

"What are possible solutions for this problem? What will remedy the situation?" (they generate solutions)

Step 6: Reassemble members and have them share their recommendations. Encourage other members to comment and add their ideas. Select the best ideas and implement them.

Step 7: Ask members to return to their subgroups briefly to complete any action plans that might be needed to make sure that improvements are implemented.

Priority Setting

What is it? A process for involving the members of a team or department in identifying priorities in a budget or programming cutback situation.

When should you use it? When there is a desire to involve the members of the group rather than having management determine the priorities. To benefit from the input and ideas of all staff.

What is its purpose? Helps members clarify their priorities and take responsibility for managing in a constrained environment.

What is the outcome? A set of priorities created by group members which they're prepared to accept and to which they have a high level of commitment.

How does Priority Setting work?

Step 1: Identify the parameters of the priority-setting

exercise. Is it to reduce budgets by 20 percent? Is it to reduce the number of products or services offered from dozens to three or four? Is it to simplify an operation? Also, clarify the timelines and other realities.

If there are implications for job loss or job reassignment, these issues must be discussed openly at the start of the exercise.

Step 2: Identify all of the items that will be the focus of the priority-setting exercise. These could range from products and services to publications and office locations.

Step 3: Work together to create a list of criteria for assessing the relative importance of these items. This priority-setting criteria should be created by the group to fit the specific situation. Five to seven criteria usually will suffice.

Examples include the following:
- meets customer needs/ expectations
- supports the strategic direction
- has top level support
- aligns with political priorities
- creates economic benefits
- creates social benefits
- creates environmental benefits
- creates high profile
- represents a major innovation
- is doable/feasible
- positive cost/benefit ratio
- has positive impact on staff
- contributes to program balance

Step 4: Once the criteria have been identified, construct a grid with the items to be prioritized down the left-hand column and the criteria across the top. Rate each item using a scale to reflect the extent to which it meets the criteria.

The following example uses a numerical scale where 1 = low priority, 2 = medium priority, and 3 = high priority.

Example: If the zoo cuts its programs, what aspects should remain?

	Meets Needs of Public	Supports Strategic Direction	Creates Economic Direction	Positive Cost/ Benefit Benefits	Total Rating Ratio
Children's petting zoo	3	3	3	2.5	11.5
Guided tours	2	1	2	1	6
Guest speakers	1.75	2.5	1	1	6.25
Zoo magazine for kids	2.5	3	2	1	8.5

Step 5: Openly discuss each item in detail before individuals rate them. Since the final decision is made through individual ranking, this group discussion is essential. It's especially important if jobs are at stake. In some priority-setting exercises it may be advantageous to 'weight' the criteria. For details see pg. 147, in this chapter.

Step 6: Members then rank the items according to their understanding of how well each item meets the criteria.

Step 7: The scores are added, divided by the number of raters and results discussed. Discussion questions include, *"Did the right priorities emerge? What are the scores telling us?"*

Step 8: The results of a priority-setting exercise can then be referred to a subcommittee of the larger group. It's this group's responsibility to translate the priorities into actual budget numbers and create an implementation plan. The final plan should be fed back to the whole group for their ratification if the process is to remain participative.

Needs and Offers Negotiation

What is it? A constructive dialogue between two parties to identify action steps each can take to improve the relationship.

When should you use it? To encourage dialogue between parties either to resolve a conflict or to proactively improve relations before problems set in.

What is its purpose? Resolves issues in a relatively low-risk manner because issues are framed as positive suggestions for improvement by both parties.

What is the outcome? A positive and constructive dialogue that lets people express past and present concerns about the relationship in totally constructive terms. Since both parties make offers, the exchange feels mutual and supportive.

How does Needs and Offers Negotiation work?

Step 1: Clarify who will be the focus of the exercise. This can be two separate parties: a team and its leader, two subgroups of the same team, a team and management, or two individuals.

Step 2: Set a positive climate for the exercise by talking about the value of giving and receiving feedback. Make sure that the appropriate norms are in place to encourage members to speak freely and honestly.

Step 3: Explain the process to all parties. Instruct parties that they will be separated for a period of about 20 minutes. During that time each party will think about the following:

- What I/we need from you in order to be effective
- What I/we offer in return to meet your needs.

Write the results of the deliberations on a flip chart.

The following example is from an exchange between a team and its leader.

Needs	Offers
What I/we need from you in order to be effective	*What I/we offer in return to meet your needs*
• More advance notice about program changes	• Full and active participation at staff meetings
• More consultation about changes that affect staff	• Getting work done on time
• Clarity regarding how much authority we have to implement	• More advance communication if things are going wrong

Step 4: When each party has written its wants/offers lists, bring parties back together to share their thoughts.

Step 5: Ask each party to withhold any comments or reactions while the other person or group presents their wants and offers. When finished, discuss their reactions. Help groups work out the action steps.

Step 6: To conclude, ask each party to make a summary statement about what their commitments and action steps will be. Put in place a process for follow-up actions.

Systematic Problem Solving

What is it? A step-by-step approach for resolving a problem or issue.

When should you use it? When members need to work together to resolve a problem.

What is its purpose? Provides a structured and disciplined means for groups to explore and resolve an issue together. An in-depth analysis ensures that groups understand their problem before jumping to solutions. This is probably the most fundamental and important facilitator tool you can employ!

What is the outcome? Systematic problem solving results in doable action steps that members of the group take responsibility for implementing. Because the process is systematic, it stops the group from randomly suggesting ideas that never get implemented. Problem solving is at the heart of collaborative conflict resolution. It's also a key activity in any organization that is dedicat-

ed to improving customer service and continuous
improvement.

How does Systematic Problem-Solving work

Step 1: Name the problem. Identify a problem that
needs to be solved. Analyze it briefly to ensure that
there is a common understanding of the issue, then sup
port the group in writing a one or two sentence
description of the problem. This is called the problem
statement.

Step 2: Identify the goal of the problem-solving exercise. Ask the group one of the following questions: *"If
this problem were totally solved, how would you describe the
ideal situation"* or *"How will things look if we solve this prob
lem?"* Summarize this in a one to two sentence goal
statement.

Step 3: Analyze the problem. If the problem is fairly
technical, do an analysis using a Fishbone Diagram (pg.
145). Otherwise, ask a series of probing questions to
help members think analytically about the problem.
Categorize the observations as either 'causes' or 'effect
The goal is to get to the true root causes of the problem

Some useful questions during analysis could include:

• Describe this problem to me in detail, step by step
• What is it? How does it manifest itself?
• What are the noticeable signs of it?
• What makes this happen?
• How are people affected?

- What other problems does it cause?
- What are the most damaging aspects?
- What stops us from solving it?
- Who gets in the way of solving it?
- What are the root causes of each symptom?

Step 4: Identify potential solutions. Use Brainstorming (pg. 134) or Nominal Group Technique (pg. 136) to generate potential solutions. When the ideas stop flowing, ask probing questions to encourage members to dig deeper. Some useful probing questions include:

- What if money were no object?
- What if you owned this company?
- What would the customer suggest?
- What if we did the opposite of the ideas suggested so far?
- What is the most innovative thing we could do?

Step 5: Evaluate solutions. Use either a Criteria-Based Grid (pg. 147) or the Impact/Effort-Based Grid (pg. 148) to sift through the brainstormed ideas and determine which are most applicable to the situation.

Step 6: Create an action plan. Spell out the specific steps needed to implement the best solutions. Specify how things will be done, when and by whom.

Each action step should also have some sort of a performance indicator that answers the question, *"How will we know we have been successful?"* This indicator will help focus the action step and make it easier to measure results later on.

Step 8: Troubleshoot the plan. Use the Troubleshooting Worksheet (pg. 169) to identify all of the things that could get in the way and then make sure that there are plans in place to deal with them.

Step 9: Monitor and evaluate. Identify how the action plans will be monitored and when and how the results will be reported. Create and use a monitoring and report-back format.

You will notice that Systematic Problem Solving incorporates many of the basic facilitation process tools.

Systematic Problem-Solving Worksheet #1

Step 1: Name the problem

Identify the problem that needs to be solved. Analyze it in just enough detail to create a common understanding. Use the space below to explore the general nature of the problem.

Now narrow in and select the specific aspect you wish to solve. Write a one or two sentence problem statement to clearly define the problem.

Problem statement:

_____

_____

_____

Systematic Problem-Solving Worksheet #2

Step 2: Identify the goal of the problem-solving exercise

Describe the desired outcome. What would things look like if the problem disappeared? How would things look if the problem were resolved? Use the space below to record the ideas generated.

Now narrow in and write a one or two sentence goal statement.

Goal statement:

Systematic Problem-Solving Worksheet #3

Step 3: Analyze the problem

Dissect the problem thoroughly. Avoid coming up with solutions. Instead, concentrate on making sure that everyone is clear about the specific nature of the situation. Don't focus on symptoms, but delve behind each effect to determine the root causes.

Use Cause and Effect Charting or a Fishbone Diagram (pg.#___) if the problem is a complex technical issue that has many contributing factors.

If you decide to use a simple questioning approach, ask these questions:

- How would we describe this problem to an outsider?
- What is taking place? What are the signs and symptoms?
- How are people affected? What makes this happen?
- What are the root causes of each symptom?
- What other problems does it cause?
- What are the most damaging aspects?
- What and who stops us from solving it?
- How do we contribute to the problem?

Systematic Problem-Solving Worksheet #4

Step 4: Identify potential solutions

Use Brainstorming (pg. 134) or the Nominal Group Technique (p. 135) to generate a list of potential solutions to the problem.

When brainstorming, remember the rules:
- let the ideas flow, be creative, don't judge
- all ideas accepted, even if they're way-out
- build on the good ideas of others

Probing questions to ask once the group has run out of ideas:
- What if money were no object?
- What if I owned this company?
- What would the customer suggest?
- What's the opposite of something already suggested?
- What is the most innovative thing we could do?

Record brainstorming ideas here:

Systematic Problem-Solving Worksheet #5

Step 5: Evaluate the solutions

Use Impact/Effort -Based Grid to sift through the brainstormed ideas and determine which are best for the situation.

	– Effort –	
	Difficult To Do	Easy To Do
Major Improvement	3.	1.
Minor Improvement	4.	2.

– Impact –

List all of the type 1 & 2 activities together for quick action	List all of the type 3 activities here for development into action plans

Systematic Problem-Solving Worksheet #6

Step 6: Plan for action

Create detailed action plans for items that need to be implemented. Make sure action plans adhere to a logical sequence of steps. Provide details about what will be done, how and by whom. Always put in target dates for completion. Identify the performance indicator that answers the question, "How will we know we did a good job?"

What will be done & how?	By whom?	When?	Performance Indicator

Systematic Problem-Solving Worksheet #7

Step 7: Troubleshoot the action plan

Identify all of the things that could get in the way of success in implementing the plan. Create anticipatory strategies to deal with each of the serious blockages.

Use the following questions to help identify trouble spots:

- *What are the most difficult, complex or sensitive aspects of our plan?*
- *What sudden shifts could take place to change priorities or other wise change the environment?*
- *What organizational blocks and barriers could we run into?*
- *What technical or materials-related problems could stop or delay us?*
- *Should we be aware of any human resources issues? Which ones?*
- *In which ways might members of this team not fulfill their commitments?*

What could go wrong, block us or change suddenly?	What actions do we need to take to overcome each block? (what, how, by whom, when)

Systematic Problem-Solving Worksheet #8

Step 8: Monitor and evaluate

To ensure that action plans are actually implemented, identify the following:

How will progress be reported? Written _____ Verbal _____

When and how often will reports be made? _____

Who needs to be advised?_____

How will results be monitored?_____

Will there be a final report? _____

Who will take responsibility for the above actions? _____

_____

Reporting on Results

What activities have been implemented?	What results have been achieved?
Remaining items	Expected dates for completion

Notes

You can order from either: **Participative DYNAMICS**

or

AQP

Participative Dynamics

<u>USA</u>
Phone: 888-358-8848
Fax: 888-358-8840
Mail:
6944 W. Country Club Drive N.,
Sarasota, Florida. 34243

<u>Canada</u>
Phone: 888-465-9494
Fax: 888-465-8998
Mail:
110 Gough Street,
Toronto, Ontario. M4K 3N8

AQP

Phone- 800-733-331
Fax- 513-381-0070
Mail:
801-B West 8th Stre
Suite 501,
Cincinnati, Ohio
45203-1607

Shipping/Handling Charges & Taxes:	**Price per copy:**	
Will be a minimum of $5.00 or 5% (whichever is greater). Any applicable taxes will be extra.	1-9	$ 7.95
	10-49	$ 6.95
	50-99	$ 6.50
	100-499	$ 5.95
	500 +	*Call us!*

Payment Methods
We accept payment by check, money order or credi
card. Purchase orders are also accepted. If you are
paying by purchase order, please provide the name
and address of the person to be billed and send a
copy of the P.O. when ordering.

1. Shipping Address (We cannot ship to a P. O. Box)

Contact Name: _____
Organization: _____
Address: _____
City: _____ State/Prov: _____
Zip: _____
Phone: ( ) _____ Fax: ( ) _____

2. Quantity & Price

Book	Quantity	Unit Price	Total Price
Facilitating at a Glance!			
Applicable Tax			
Shipping/Handling			
Total			

3. Payment Method

❏ Check enclosed: $ _____
❏ Credit Card #: _____ Exp. _____
       Signature: _____
❏ Purchase order #: _____
Bill to: _____
Address: _____
City/State/Zip: _____

Thank you for your order!

The Facilitator's Process at a Glance

To start a facilitation
- welcome participants
- introduce members
- explain your role
- clarify session goal
- ratify agenda
- explain the process
- set time frames
- appoint time keeper
  and minute taker
- start the discussion

Remember to:
• stay neutral
• make eye contact
• include quiet people
• paraphrase actively
• weave their ideas together
• ask probing questions
• park off-topic items
• watch the time
• refer questions back to them

During a facilitation
- ask "How's this going?"
- check the pace: too fast,
  too slow?
- check if the techniques
  are working
- take the pulse of
  members
- summarize periodically
  and at end of session

Manage Conflict by:
1. Venting feelings:
• listen
• empathize
• clarify
2. Resolving the issue:
• take a problem-solving
approach and end with clear
action steps

To end a facilitation
- help members make a
  clear statement of
  what was decided
- develop clear next
  steps with dates
  and names
- round up leftover items
- help create next agenda
- clarify follow-up process
- evaluate the session

Tool Kit
Visioning
Sequential questioning
Brainstorming
Priority Setting
Forcefield Analysis
Multi-Voting
Root-Cause Analysis
Decision Grids
Troubleshooting
Systematic Problem Solving

Be Soft on People – Hard on Issues!